CHRI

JOHANN SEBASTIAN BACH

RICK MARSCHALL

THOMAS NELSON
Since 1798

NASHVILLE   DALLAS   MEXICO CITY   RIO DE JANEIRO

Published in Nashville, Tennessee, by Thomas Nelson. Thomas Nelson is a registered trademark of Thomas Nelson, Inc.

Published in association with the literary agency of WordServe Literary Group, Ltd., 10152 S. Knoll Circle, Highlands Ranch, Colorado, 80130.

Thomas Nelson, Inc., titles may be purchased in bulk for educational, business, fund-raising, or sales promotional use. For information, please e-mail SpecialMarkets@ThomasNelson.com.

Library of Congress Cataloging-in-Publication Data

Marschall, Richard.
  Johann Sebastian Bach / Rick Marschall.
    p. cm. -- (Christian encounters)
  Includes bibliographical references and index.
  ISBN 978-1-59555-108-5 (alk. paper)
  1. Bach, Johann Sebastian, 1685-1750--Religion. 2. Composers--Germany--
      Biography. I. Title.
ML410.B1M284 2011
780.92--dc22
  [B]   2010042812

Printed in the United States of America

11 12 13 14 15 HCI 6 5 4 3 2 1

To the memory of my parents,

Martin Hermann and Grace Lohse Marschall.

Ein feste Burg ist unser Gott.

CONTENTS

INTRODUCTION

Jesu, juva

Johann Sebastian Bach's most recent biographer, Christoph Wolff—who surely is the best thing to befall Bach since the revivals of harpsichords and "period instrument" performances—has said that "Bach's biography suffers from a serious lack of information on details" and that "his music . . . is a much stronger and more important presence." As we shall see, the "learned musician" and musical "Fifth Evangelist" was, indeed, remarkably indifferent to introspection. The author of the most monumental of the Bach biographies, Philipp Spitta, wrote in 1873, "It is quite certain that Bach rarely wrote letters, most rarely of all to private persons." Since Bach's music overwhelms us even more over the centuries, there is not a total vacuum—we almost seem to know Bach *through* his music.

We cannot doubt that Bach would be quite satisfied with this state of biographical affairs. "You want to discern a personality in my music?" we can perhaps hear him asking. "Listen closer and you will find one—the Lord Jesus Christ."

To the extent I have rightly judged his elusive personality, I have rejoiced that there *is* so much to share. First, he was an intensely spiritual man. Second, he devoted his massive talent to the God he believed graced him with it. Third, by the career choices Bach made—the musical realms he did *not* enter—he managed to write diaries-of-sorts for our perusal. From those "footprints," plus the records he did leave of minor daily preoccupations and petty disputes with town councils, an interesting, genuine portrait emerges.

Biographies of Bach cannot fail to mention, or even dwell on, Christian music. It would be like telling the life story of Charles Schulz without mentioning that *Peanuts* thing. Yet there have been very few studies on Bach's faith life—the *Christian encounters* he experienced and precipitated—and I pray that this book fills that need.

It is not necessary to be a learned musician, nor a Bible scholar, to discover the man Bach, the servant of God, in these pages. It is only desirable that you have a healthy curiosity for a time very different from our own, an appreciation for evidence of God's workings in the hearts and creativity of yielded servants, and a willingness to be inspired by one of mankind's astonishing figures.

My introduction to Johann Sebastian Bach and Baroque music was in my home. My father played a lot of it on his hi-fi in the 1950s, just as he played a lot of jazz and opera. None of it was forced on me, which enabled me to fall in love with

Bach without coercion. Both sides of my family were strong German Lutherans, so I was destined, perhaps, to write at least this introduction.

Baroque music was "rediscovered" during my childhood. It was a big deal when Vivaldi's *Four Seasons* burst on the scene and when Leonard Bernstein, of all people, conducted it. On New York radio, the eccentric DeKoven on WRVR—advocating his patented "Barococo" music—and the grumpy Watson overnight on WNCN, shared literally unheard-of musical treasures. The Record Hunter, a store on Fifth Avenue, had a "mole" who phoned my father and his friend, Henry James, whenever a shipment of European vinyl arrived. Similarly, as fellow students of mine slipped into movie theaters or upstate taverns, I would grab every opportunity to go to Manhattan for concerts and recitals of Baroque music.

My mother reminded me always of the content of Bach's music. "Listen to the words; read the translation-sheets; remember why he composed them!" Those seeds have sprouted on these pages.

When I was a teenager I explained my love for Baroque music as fascination that such emotion could derive from within a straitjacket. Not that I have ever sought therapy, but I shared the attitude of contemporary composer Michael Torke, who said: "Why waste money on psychotherapy when you can listen to the *B minor Mass*?" Eventually I realized that the compelling aspects were the structure itself—yes, the straitjacket—and the spiritual content, not just the emotional buttons that were pushed by pleasant melodies.

Years later I was a guest on a Public Radio station in Connecticut. The program was called "A Man and His Music," and I was the guest because I had written a few books, including some on country music. I was asked to choose some cuts and discuss the reasons for my affection. Many of my favorite pieces were from Christian music—many by Mozart and, of course, Bach. When I brought the discussion around to explain the texts and what the spiritual contents meant to me, the host hurried me along.

The same prejudice, overt or subtle, shrouds Bach's music in many quarters today. Our culture tends to listen to his works as concert pieces; there often is a benign neglect of their intense spirituality. Without awareness of that aspect we cannot fully appreciate his life, nor really understand the music. Herein I aim to correct that. Bach, an icon in history, has come to be real to me. And I hope, as you read this book, he becomes real to you too.

Rick Marschall

A BRIGHT SUNRISE

Music has been mandated by God's Spirit.

—Johann Sebastian Bach

The music of Johann Sebastian Bach is hard to study, but easy to understand.

In a manner of speaking, that can be said of his life too. He was born more than three centuries ago, a time whose fashions, whose daily habits, and certainly whose musical styles, are not familiar to us today. Bach occasionally justified the characterization that he could be irritable and demanding, a prototypical "artistic temperament." He was the father of twenty children; he never traveled more than a few hundred miles from his birthplace; he wrote music that, by the end of his life, was widely viewed as complicated and theoretical, inaccessible and dense.

Yet he was totally transparent. And if his music is easy to understand, his faith is even more so: without guile, self-evident, and inspiring—if we let it be. Music was Bach's life—his talent a gift from God, he believed. He sought to praise God by making his church music to be sermons in song. He knew the Bible so well that he was the functional equivalent of pastor in positions he held. He saw his "secular" music equally as honoring to God as his church works. And what works they all were! Almost twelve hundred compositions of all sorts have arrived—organ and keyboard works, suites, concertos, even a complex fugue masterfully built on the letters of his name; and church music, including cantatas, Masses, motets, musical Passions, songs, and hymns. Bach's Christian music served as forcefully—and to the same ends—as the creeds, Bible readings, and sermons with which they were nestled in church services.

St. Paul's epistles can be read, but only read. Luther's powerful sermons fill many volumes, but they, too, can only be read today. Theologians, evangelists, and preachers from centuries of Christianity's heritage move our spirits today—through their words. Bach, too, was a preacher, as effective and doctrinally pure as many saints since apostolic times, but he exhorted through his music. Those sermons in music live today, ministering to our ears and emotions but also to our minds and hearts. Indeed, to our souls.

The simple life he led (by the way, to most observers one of modesty and thoroughgoing affability) was in stark contrast to the complex music he composed and performed. Is Bach's music profound or simple? It is both. He was a man of the austere Baroque period, yet his music touches the soul more directly, and more humanly, than that of any composer of the Romantic period. The humanity and passion of his work is what breathed life into otherwise restrictive forms.

Newcomers to his music—indeed, newcomers to his remarkable life, which was surrendered to a continuous passion to honor God—can choose to be bewildered by the quaint aspects of earlier times, the unfamiliar initial sounds of Bach's music. Or they can let the sheer audacity of magnificence pour over them; they can luxuriate in the talent of a God-ordained musical servant.

Johann Sebastian Bach lived during the Age of Enlightenment. Today, schoolbooks imply that this era was so named because societies "woke up" from superstition and musty traditions, most of them from "close-minded" religion, and entered a new consciousness of science, progress, and freedom. In fact, the very standard-bearers of Enlightenment thinking, beginning with the greatest scientist of the age and perhaps any age, Isaac Newton, understood Enlightenment to mean new lights shining upon our understanding of God's nature. They were "enlightened" to draw closer *to* God, not be liberated *from* Him. Science proved to them God's perfect ways of working. Political revolutions like America's were based on biblical principles, almost as if by blueprint. Art that rejoiced in nature was meant to indicate a refreshed connection with the Creator. And that included music.

The most profound composer of his age, Johann Sebastian

Bach, of the area now comprising provincial northern Germany, was a product of his times, but also of his place. There was no German state until 1871, when Kaiser Wilhelm I and Prince Otto von Bismarck united a bewildering array of principalities and free states. Beyond those political boundaries, areas like Austria, East Prussia, Alsace, parts of Bohemia, and so forth, have often been included in "German" cultural discussions. A common culture was bound, if not always by religion, then by ethnicity and language. The south was generally Catholic after the Thirty Years' War, the north generally Lutheran, and by such matrix we consider Bach's lands of Thuringia and Saxony as of northern Germany.

Bach's every composition and performance was a testament to his close relationship with God, yet he plainly termed his work "the science of music." Thus do we see in those fertile lands the conjunction of tradition, piety, a frank reliance on faith, and an intellectual Enlightenment Age thirst for artistic expression.

Isaac Newton's ideas were well known in the superficially peasant lands of Saxony and Thuringia, and it is significant that what Newton was to science and physics, Bach was to music. Essentially they both sought to prove that their works, their discoveries, their observations—and all the implications they drew—illuminate the workings of a supreme Creator in the universe. Newton asserted that his numerous and astonishing discoveries "pointed to the operations of God," just as the astronomer Kepler had observed about music that it "mirrored the harmony of the universe," and in so saying he picked up the philosophic thread from Plato who recognized in musical harmony a reflection of the Golden Ideal, a certain set of universal truths. The Enlightenment connected the dots between Pythagoras and Plato to Copernicus and Kepler, adding a biblical perspective to observations about universal harmony and perfection. Plato, who lived before Christ, in fact was embraced by early fathers of the church. His attitudes, certainly as regards absolute truth and music's effect on the soul, lived once again in the Age of Enlightenment. The God of Bach's age was a creator and sustainer, but also a motivator and inspirer.

This perspective allows us to see how much more than calendar years separate the cultures of earlier times and ours. We can gain a fresh view of the era that spanned the High Renaissance (roughly the generations following the artistic explosions centered in Florence and the spiritual explosions of the Reformation in Germany), the Baroque (roughly 1600–1750), and past Bach (1685–1750) to the Rococo (1750–1775) and early Classical periods (the early nineteenth century). These were times of petty wars, of plagues and famines, of gaudy opulence in European courts, and of grinding poverty and ignorance in city streets and country villages.

Specifically to Bach's own life and time, it was the back-flush of the Thirty Years' War, which ended a generation (thirty-seven years) before his birth. Incredible devastation followed one of the most useless of many useless European wars. It was fought mostly on German soil. The regions of Thuringia and Saxony were two prime objects of the combatants' desires. The Thirty Years' War was partly a result of the death throes of the Holy Roman Empire, as well as the clear establishment of Protestantism as more than a localized protest movement. It also was a fight over valuable trade routes, rich farming and mining lands, access to seaports, and more.

Spain, for instance, desired to hold to lands in the Netherlands and Italy. Denmark and Sweden coveted German lands adjacent to the Baltic Sea. France desired German soil, but also, despite being a Catholic nation and suppressing the Protestant Huguenots, resented the power of the Catholic Holy Roman Empire and therefore allied itself with Protestant Sweden. Britain had backed several factions and bankrolled war machines in the hopes of gaining leverage, but withdrew when she virtually bankrupted her empire and was overwhelmed by her own internecine conflicts. There were rivalries between the Hapsburg and Bourbon thrones, and, of course, the smoldering differences between Catholics and Protestants, the Reformation and Counter-Reformation and, yes, the Counter-Counter-Reformation.

The religious disputes had long ceased to be debates over the primacy of the pope or the doctrine of consubstantiation. By the early eighteenth century, battles raged more over the political boundaries and prerogatives of states that had declared for or against Romanism. The last of several treaties of the Thirty Years' War was signed in 1648, as opponents collapsed from exhaustion. Ironically, the supposed motivating cause of the conflicts—Catholicism versus Lutheranism—was almost a moot point, because other Protestant sects, chiefly Calvinism and Pietism, had emerged as rivals in both Catholic and Protestant lands. (Basically, the followers of John Calvin focused on predestination, the individual's inability to initiate regeneration, and a relative independence of local churches' governance. Pietists stressed personal holiness and pushed back against religious rituals. Both movements, *contra* Catholicism and Lutheranism, discouraged music in service, particularly the rise of exuberant and sophisticated expression in Bach's time.)

Treaties after the Thirty Years' War generally stipulated that monarchs could establish "state" religions of their preference within their domains but allow religious freedom to other subjects of theirs. In the German lands, comprised of 225 states, cross-border commerce and travel was common, so freedom suddenly thrived behind a very thin façade of monarchical supremacy.

Battles of this war had been fought in many places (eventually even in colonies like Brazil) but none so fiercely nor so often as on the soil of Thuringia and Saxony. In Brandenburg, the province just east of Saxony, half of the total population was killed. The Swedish armies destroyed approximately a third of all German communities—two thousand castles, fifteen hundred towns. The male population of all the German states, by some estimates, was reduced by half. Armed conflict, pillaging and looting, mercenary armies, expropriation, and expulsion of entire communities contributed to the death tolls in persecuted Germany.

Exacerbating these horrors, inevitably, were starvation and disease. The bubonic plague raged through parts of Europe at this time; dysentery and typhus were commonplace.

As armies of the Holy Roman Empire and the Danes made a battlefield of Thuringia and Saxony, the local population suffered infestations of bizarre maladies called "head disease," "Hungarian disease," and a "spotted" disease now thought to be typhus.

This was the world into which Johann Sebastian Bach was born—or rather, into which the previous generation had been born. So the culture was returning to "normal" when little Bach was growing up. Historians have reported many accounts of the dispirited population exhibiting widespread malaise after the war. Justly so. But historians have not always credited those peoples' faith in God as a palliative—no, a curative—especially when added to the traditional religious strength and cultural maturity of the north Germans, as the society revived. A long-held historical analysis suggested an additional reason for the Saxons' capacity for restoration, inherent in what was called the "germ theory": that a unique societal rejuvenation, indeed democracy itself, grew from the Saxon forests of Germany. This theory was current in late-nineteenth-century America, which romanticized that a unique combination of heartiness, self-reliance, independence, reverence, and homely virtues planted the "seed" of democracy as harvested, ultimately, in England and America.[1]

The deeply held Christian beliefs, and specifically the tenets of its native son Martin Luther, were surely the foundation stones of a spiritual revival, and other reinvigoration, amongst the peoples of Thuringia and Saxony. In the villages set amid rolling hills and dense forests, exciting ideas and political ferment rapidly took hold. The lands experienced rising literacy and increasing liberty, the spreading availability of music and art, economic renewal that afforded tradesmen (and a growing middle class) certain degrees of independence and leisure never known in Europe.

It became, with determination, a time of optimism, liberty, and artistic expression. And faith. As everywhere in Christian Europe, towns and cities of Bach's regions were built, spiritually and physically, around the church. Matters of faith and doctrine were matters serious enough over which to wage war. But in a literal sense chapels, churches, basilicas, and cathedrals were the centers of every community, not just where people worshiped, but where people met at other times for meetings and speeches; baptisms, weddings, and funerals; and at designated times for concerts, feasts, and festivals.

In Bach's day, town halls and commercial establishments also arose. Economic revival and the growing independence of the middle class led to a social network of public gardens, shops, town squares, and taverns. Craft guilds and trade associations established magnet centers and agencies. Public and private charity rivaled that of the churches. Confraternities often served as quasi-legal or para-governments, deciding disputes, providing employment, and offering a basic safety net for many citizens.

Areas like Thuringia and Saxony developed a peasant nobility—comfortable, not ostentatious; homes of solid wood furniture, for instance, not the finely carved appointments of the French; heavy tankards, not fine glassware. Yet even in this regard a development in the region illustrates the changing culture at the time of Bach's early years. A frustrated alchemist named Böttger, spurred by the entrepreneurial Augustus the Strong of Dresden, devised a means to make delicate porcelain, leading directly to the Royal Porcelain Works in Meissen, world respected ever since.

In the emerging culture of the region, there was more respect for women than was accorded in most other parts of Europe. In France, for instance, ladies initially hosted intellectual *salons*. But it was in Germany where women received elaborate musical training and vocal instruction, performing with men in public venues and, if not in royal courts, then in numerous family circles. Which status was more elevated?

~

The eighteenth century—and nowhere more so than in Thuringia and Saxony—gave rise to the nuclear family as a social and not just relational entity. These family units embraced extremely strong expressions of faith, around each hearth as well as between neighbors. The Lutheran church served as a social unifier. The Bachs were doubly blessed because the emerging economy in northern Germany honored the *artisan* class, in contrast to France, where the nobility took rank; England, where class divisions were rigidly observed; and Italy, where a moral lassitude affected the social fabric. On the soil where two centuries later the Weimar Republic sought to establish a New Order, in Bach's time it was a place where religion and art reigned without having to rule.

Flowing from this cultural dynamic were three specific and profound changes in peoples' lives. The first was a new, limited role of the state. Let us consider what that meant to Bach. As an adult, he was an employee of princes, churches, and town governments; he was not a slave, subject, or total supplicant. Second was the civic manifestation of Protestantism—the elevation of the common man. In Bach's case that led to a degree of independence and self-determination, no matter how much he chose to adhere to tradition and form. Third, rising literacy.[2] Nowhere was this more marked than in the peasant aristocracy of Thuringia and Saxony's landscape. To read the entire Bible several times during one's life was an assumption of Protestant Germans.

The nature of Lutheranism was the glue that brought, and held, these impulses together, and accelerated them. An emphasis on the individual's relationship with God (that is, recognizing no intermediary but Christ) obliged every person to be thoroughly grounded in the Word. Admonitions to personal piety, whether orthodox Lutheran or the new Pietism of Bach's day, taught believers to carry integrity and modesty into all realms of life. The high artistic traditions of the Lutherans conditioned peoples' tastes for finer expressions of music. The "priesthood of all believers" not only removed barriers between individuals and God, but encouraged people to evangelize, participate in worship, and understand all the details and implications of the liturgy.

This personal involvement in corporate worship was in contrast to the Catholic Church, which in the seventeenth century maintained that merely to be present at Mass was sufficient. The Curé of Saint-Saveir in Lille, France, wrote, "Anyone who is present in body . . . even if he is far from the altar but provided he attends to the entire mass, fulfills the commandment; it is not necessary to see the celebrant or to hear his voice."[3]

It is likely that Sebastian Bach and his family—including his extended family of guests, boarders, and servants—gathered at least twice a day for Bible reading and prayer.[4] Included were corporate and individual reading of Scripture and psalms, discussions of Luther's Catechisms, prayers of petition and thanksgiving, and—of course—song, always song.

≈

Worship services have changed in their structures, emphases, and length since the late Reformation / High Baroque periods, and at that time Lutheran and Calvinist practices differed from each other as well. Reviewing the general aspects of church worship and liturgy is useful to understand Bach, his mission, and his work.[5] Partakers of Communion received a pastoral "evangelical absolution" of sins, as a body, after confession was offered as a congregation—a practice to avoid receiving the body and blood of Christ unworthily, since the Protestants were phasing out the *Beichtstuhl* (private confession), although allowed by Luther's *Small Catechism*. When practical (and more common in Reformed than Lutheran churches), communicants sat at long tables; the bread passed by pastoral staff on plates and the wine passed from hand to hand in a common cup.

Faith was personal—knowing the "personal" Savior was stressed, even without our contemporary evangelical branding—yet worship was communal. Those two impulses are synchronous, not in conflict, and such is the essence of evangelicalism. Bach's inheritance of these Lutheran attitudes fully informed his faith. No less characteristic was his modesty in the exercise of the exceptional musical talents he was to manifest. Music, dedicated to God, was more important than Bach's own celebrity, or—to use a concept not even in use then—his ego.

Compared to other musical celebrities past and present, we find scarcely a word of boasting, reflection, self-criticism, or even analysis in Bach's papers. He wrote few letters, at least few that survived, except those seeking commissions or tangling with bureaucrats. He evidently kept no diaries or journals. *Livres de raison*—personal records of activities and motivations, a fashion of the day—were not Bach's style. He organized many musical instructions but they were to be lessons, not lectures; practice, not pontification. When he addressed musical theory, he wrote music itself, not treatises *about* the music. He did not preach about music. His music preached about Christ. Regarding music, he just *did*—recalling one of medieval theologians' attributes of the Divine: pure act.

Three strains of Protestantism were abroad in the land as Bach reached maturity, Lutheranism the dominant, yet his work was to reflect the other two in creative ways.

As a true disciple of Luther he strove to absorb, compose, and live the doctrines of confessional orthodoxy [traditional Lutheran], the devotional and active faith of the pietists, and the spiritual union with Christ sought after by the mystics [a school of pastors and artists who stressed contemplation, creative/artistic expression of their faith, and private spirituality—we might say the north German, Protestant, Baroque version of monasticism]—all of whom expressed some worthy aspirations for any Christian.[6]

Bach began virtually every composition, even his secular music, with a blank paper on which he wrote, *Jesu, juva* (Jesus, help me) on the upper left corner of the first page and *Soli Deo Gloria* (To God alone the glory) on the bottom right corner of the completed score. His was a personal relationship, not a professional duty, with the Savior.

Such "bookends" were as anointing oil over all of Bach's creative work. So did he begin and end his days—and his life—with such petition and praise: "Jesus, help me" and "To God alone be all the glory." With or without the mode of music, such dedication speaks to us through the years of Bach's relevance today.

FERTILE SOIL

For the glory of the most high God alone, And for my neighbor to learn from.

—Johann Sebastian Bach

I magine yourself able to fly through time, to knock on the doors of homes where newborn babies lay, speaking to parents of famous musical composers and musicians from different times, different countries, different musical styles; to ask if they could imagine that their baby would grow up to be the greatest composer in the world's history.

It is not difficult to imagine certain reactions. Mozart's father, a respected but minor court and chapel composer, would have wished that it be so (and, after Bach, his case comes the closest). Beethoven's father was also in the music business, but was a sluggard of mediocre talent and less ambition; he would have been surprised at your news. Händel was the son of a barber. Haydn the son of a wagon maker. The father of Gluck, the prodigious composer of operas, had hoped his son would become a forester like himself. Wagner's father was a petty bureaucrat. Verdi was born into poverty, not any musical tradition. And so on.

But different it would be to knock on the door of Johann Ambrosius Bach in the little German town of Eisenach just after March 21, 1685, and predict that *his* newborn son was destined to be the greatest music maker of the human race. He might call out the news to his wife, Elizabeth Lämmerhirt, and then warmly invite you in for a drink or a meal. That is to say, it might not have surprised the *Stadtpfeiffer* (town musician), because the Bachs could trace many musicians and composers in their family, going back a century and spread across four crowded branches of the family tree. The family was so associated with music that, in one area, town musicians were nicknamed "bachs" even after there were no Bachs among them. Many of these men, including Johann Sebastian's uncles and older cousins, held respectable places in musical history without his eventual luster casting a glow upon their names.

Music: it was what the Bachs *did*. Farmers worked the soil, bakers baked, millers ground grain, smiths worked with iron. The Bachs wrote music, made music, transcribed music, performed music, taught music, *breathed* music. Little Johann Sebastian will grow up to command the world's attention with his music? *Warum nicht?* (Why not?)

We have a feel for the culture into which Bach was born, on the rebound from a devastating war. Humble, faithful, cultured, proud, and alive with faith in God. The French call it *bourgeois*. Germans, alluding to their gift of amiable simplicity, use the words *Gemeinschaft* (often translated as "community") for the culture and *Gemütlichkeit* for the atmosphere of hospitality of the home. Martin Luther democratized many aspects of religious expression, not the least of which were substituting German for Latin in the service and the generous use of music in worship. It is curious and significant that the lives of Luther and Bach were so intertwined, although roughly two centuries divided them.

Luther was not born in Eisenach, but he was reared there. He was educated at the local school where Bach was to study. When Luther was pursued and persecuted for his faith, he returned to Eisenach to hide. There, in the mighty Wartburg Castle in whose shadow Johann Sebastian Bach was born and where he was baptized, Martin Luther translated the New Testament into German, the language of the people. This work, in Eisenach, ignited a revolution whose aspects were spiritual, political, and cultural. And intimately precious to the souls of Christ-followers.

Eisenach and the Wartburg Castle had been associated with music since at least 1207, when the Tourney of Song, a "highpoint of German minstrelsy"[1] was held there. Bach, even through his days in the esteemed city of Leipzig, a capital of culture and commerce, was to remain a lifelong citizen of Eisenach (population approximately six thousand) in peasant pride and a palpable identification with music and Lutheran roots. So it is more than metaphor that Bach grew up in Luther's shadow.

And a great musical tradition, fostered by Luther, cast part of that great shadow. The role of music in the church is a topic that provides a foundational understanding of spiritual and social impulses behind the Reformation. The ebb and flow of sanction, disapproval, encouragement, and restrictions on music through the centuries is a laundry list of inconsistencies. "Bach always understood his positions as Cantor, Music Director, and Organist to be offices founded by King David in I Chronicles," according to music historian Paul S. Jones. "As such, he took the role very seriously and served as a dedicated, empowered leader within the church hierarchy."[2] Worship music *sacrosanct*? The origin of that word is "doubly holy"—sacred by holy sanction. Yet it was not always so, or even invariably so.

Bach was blessed in most of his postings to have lavish resources, the approval of churches, and budgets wherewith to excel. He wrote margin notes in his Bible about King David, joyful noises, and tambourines. But in the larger Christian tradition, only in the second century was the ground widely prepared for music in worship; this despite Paul's recommendations of joyful music in his letters to believers in Ephesus and Colosse.

St. Cecilia died a martyr with a song on her lips and became revered as the patron saint of music. St. Ambrose (born in Germany in the fourth century) introduced hymnody to the liturgy. After Ambrose and Augustine, congregations sang limited songs: the doxology, amens, the kyrie, and primitive hymns. At the end of the sixth century, the gaggle of Gregorian "reforms" forbad singing in the Mass, except by priests. Yet in German churches (already displaying independence of papal decrees) local congregations continued to allow congregants to sing alle-lujahs and the kyrie. "Sequences," often in local tongues, were sung by the worshipers.

Through the centuries more congregational singing became standard, in a random mixture of Latin and the native German tongue, prefiguring Luther's reforms. Mystery plays, religious/social celebrations that were the ancestors of Passions and ora-torios, were musical dramas featuring costumed actors as well as singers and musicians. Bach's biographer Albert Schweitzer explained:

> The Mystery Plays that had such a vogue in the fourteenth and fifteenth centuries also helped the German hymn to conquer the church. The mixed Latin-German Christmas cradle-songs have a quite uncommon charm. The poetry of them is of the most primitive kind imaginable, the words are put together less with regard to the sense than to the sound and the rocking rhythm; yet the bright Christmas enchant-ment that surrounds them affects us no less than it did the generations that have vanished.[3]

By the way, rather than identify Dr. Albert Schweitzer (1875–1965) each time we refer to him—at the risk of suggest-ing he was not one man, but septuplets—we here describe him as a German-French Alsatian, medical doctor and Lutheran pastor, respected theologian and master organist, medical missionary to central Africa (Lambaréné), and Nobel Peace Prize laureate. His detailed biography of Bach was published in French in 1904, in German in 1908, and in English in 1911, expanded in each edition. Each of his life experiences enabled a better understanding of Bach's own facets, and although his biography is relatively obscure today, it provides a unique perspective.

Between the times of Luther and the French Revolution, music played a major role in making the daily life of everyday people bearable, pleasant, even joyful. As with iPods today, it was possible for people in some places to enjoy music almost all their waking hours. This was generally true throughout Europe, and in Germany specifically.

Many villages had *Stadtpfeiffers* on the municipal payrolls —town musicians who roamed the streets, played in parks, or—imagine this—played atop towers in town squares or at the city gates. Passersby and shoppers and people from their windows could hear music played all day. Another category of music of the time was *Tafelmusik*—literally "table music"— to be performed in the background during meals. Obviously, only the wealthier citizens could arrange for this, but the musical ensembles often repeated their programs afterward in public parks, sometimes on their own and sometimes by the generosity of their patrons.

Today's rock concerts might have nothing on certain musical events of those earlier times. There is a report of an evening music concert (*Abendmusik*) at the Marienkirche in the north

German city of Lübeck in 1705.[4] Bach attended the event, a tribute to Prince Leopold. The crowds were so many, and so enthusiastic, that extra security—"two corporals and 18 privates"—had to be called out.

Musical instruction was so ubiquitous that when people gathered for social visits, the performance of some music was a communal act, with everyone participating. Women, otherwise second-class citizens in so many ways, frequently sang, received music lessons, and played keyboards, lutes, and mandolins after evening meals and at get-togethers. Bach was a strong proponent of women singing, if not always in churches, then in social situations, in weekly musical gatherings for the public.

Some composers in Germany of that time made their careers by rewriting tunes from many sources—new church music, secular concertos or chamber music, or operas—quickly setting them for small ensembles or keyboards or roving street bands of wind musicians, in an early version of each week's "Top 40." People thereby became familiar with the latest tunes, keeping them in their heads, able to hum or whistle them as they wished. Such wind ensembles became so beloved in Vienna that by the Classical era, Haydn, Mozart, Beethoven, and Hummel made sure to include identifiable wind-ensemble aspects in their symphonies and concertos. The audience was sure to be satisfied!

Another example of how church music was *everywhere*—literally—was in Salzburg at the hands of the Baroque composer Heinrich Ignaz Franz von Biber, known today as the father of mature violin technique and the haunting "Mystery

Sonatas." As the chapel composer in the Salzburg Cathedral, he once wrote a polychoral Mass that puts all later attempts at "surround sound" to shame. In that massive, sky-high cathedral, he positioned musicians and voices in fifty-three "parts" (not movements but performers—thirty-seven instrumental soloists or ensembles; sixteen solo voices or groups) in the *Missa Salisburgensis* (1682).

Biber dispersed them all in seven separate groups around the church. High and low, front and back, to the left and to the right. More than one organ. Two separate ensembles of trumpets. Loud timpani drums. Solo singers here and there, choruses in several locations. When the Mass was performed—surely no easy task to hold together—worshipers heard music and the message-in-song from every side, seemingly every corner of the great cathedral. Wherever they looked or turned their ears, music flowed forth. It was a "total experience"—perhaps a picture of countless saints praising the Lord in heaven.

Protestantism and specifically Lutheran theology and worship traditions were central to Bach's preoccupations, his composing, his life. Luther's *Small Catechism* taught reliance on Scripture and not church hierarchy; a no-frills life of service based on the Ten Commandments, the Creeds, and the Lord's Prayer; a lesser number of recognized sacraments (baptism, Communion, and confession of sin with absolution) than in the Roman rites; and the Protestants' trademark "direct lines" to God, eschewing priestly confession and any intercessors than Christ when approaching God. Corporate worship and praise—congregational singing and a heightened role for music as a means of exhortation and exposition of the gospel—were Lutheran hallmarks that Bach was to intensify and standardize.

The beauty and power—that is, the effectiveness—with which he did this confirms Bach's historical significance in religious tradition as equal to his prominence in musical history. Many observers have called him "The Fifth Evangelist."

Beyond this there is the "nationalistic" aspect of his music, without which we have an incomplete understanding of the man Johann Sebastian Bach. He did not merely join the north German "school" of composition by virtue of convenience, nor did he merely take that school to new levels. Bach's self-conscious identity as inheritor of a regional tradition was a positive motive force in his creativity, which—no coincidence—coincided with aspects of Lutheranism since its inception, and was carried thereafter into German Romanticism.

In terms of compositional techniques, Bach lived in a world of styles and approaches that he desired to perpetuate. Let the names of musical forebears suffice here. Generations of German composers preceding Bach were innovative, influential, and prolific—Ludwig Senfl, Heinrich Schütz, Heinrich Isaac, Michael Praetorius, Johann Hermann Schein, Samuel Scheidt. These, as well as numerous Bachs, were the musical heroes of Bach's youth. Instrumentation, the architecture of suites, harmonic structures—all had synthesized to a "German style."

In church music the north German traditions were no less influential. Traits include a democratization of worship and music, accessibility to the common people—the importance of the common tongue, not the otherwise remote Latin, in worship and music and liturgy. As a result, many new people, including amateurs, students, and volunteers, were drawn into worship. Also, there was an increase in congregational singing, input of church councils, and laymen's participation. In churches, all these factors were a general departure from the traditional Catholic worship at that time.

~

Despite the "German character" of Bach's music, he was open, even eager, to absorb foreign influences, a natural recipe-pattern in the development of any musical style. Jazz cannot be called African, to cite a parallel case, but it would not exist without its African antecedents. Bach was to incorporate, as well as reject, aspects of other national styles, always synthesizing. Likewise, Biber had worked in Salzburg but influenced a generation of Italian violinists. Händel moved from Lower Saxony to Italy and adopted the styles of Italian opera, then moved to London, where he became an "English" composer second to Purcell. Luigi Boccherini moved from Lucca in Tuscany to Spain and incorporated the guitar into much of his music. Composers chose their "schools," some helped define them. Bach surely did.

Unlike these other music makers, Bach kept his hometown as the lifelong center of his universe. The area surrounding little Eisenach, in Thuringia, where he was born, resembled a peasant kingdom. The Prussian court in Potsdam outside Berlin was a model of regal splendor and seemed to be a world apart.

(Indeed, the palace *Sanssouci* [Without Sorrows] was modeled after French courts.) But that is characteristic of Saxony and Thuringia of the time. Superficial refinement was borrowed from the French and Italians. Newer musical forms like concerted dances were "imported" from France to the court at Celle, Lower Saxony; operas in the Italian style were the rage in Hamburg theaters.

Yet overall, northern Germany was developing a distinctiveness; its culture incorporated, rather than substituted, outside influences. As a cradle of the Reformation, the area was one of advanced and widespread spiritual maturity. Moreover, literacy was among the highest of any part of Europe. In some Lutheran districts, church law ordered the public to learn to read "in order to 'see' God's orders and commandments," and—quoting an edict from the time of Bach's birth—"the clergy was ordered to instruct in reading skills."[5] Around the time of Bach's death, surveys of estate inventories indicated that in the German Lutheran cities of Tübingen, Speyer, and Frankfurt, books and personal libraries were listed in, respectively, 89, 88, and 79 percent of homes. (In Paris, at the same time, the figure was 22 percent.)

This characteristic was not merely national but, again, a distinctive of Lutheran culture. For instance, in the city of Metz, a 1673 survey of household estates revealed that 70 percent of Protestant households contained books, compared to 25 percent of Catholic households. Generally speaking, Calvinists encouraged literacy at comparable rates, and Pietists were probably responsible for even higher rates of literacy and acquisition of books than were the Lutherans.[6] This was the soil where Luther translated the Bible into the language of the people, and where Bach happily inherited a tradition of shedding Latin for German in the music of the church—hymns, congregational songs, motets, chorales, cantatas, oratorios, and Masses. Protestantism was having its effect on the culture and everyday life, not just on believers' souls.

Bach's profound Christian faith, grounded in deep scholarship (his library boasted as many theology texts as musical treatises), when combined with his astonishing mastery of musical form, resulted in Albert Schweitzer's awestruck characterization of Bach as a "historical postulate." He was unique not just in *his* time, but for *all* time. The historian of church music Peter Jones noted: "There are those who argue for Bach's exclusive Lutheran orthodoxy, others who claim he was a Pietist, and still others who state that he was influenced by mystic theologians. In some sense, they are all correct, for Bach was a confessional Lutheran with great personal piety who was influenced by the mystics."[7] And it is to be noted that, despite his fierce Lutheran loyalty, Bach worked for a time at a Calvinist royal court (Cöthen) and composed a German-style Mass for a Catholic court (Dresden).

≈

As *character* is defined as "actions taken when no one is looking," so was Bach's faith active and mature in his quiet moments of study. He devoted himself to more than music. One interesting piece of evidence is his famous copy of the *Calov Commentary* on Luther's translation of the Bible. Incredibly, this mammoth work—the ownership of which reveals so much about Bach's Christian scholarship—was discovered in an old trunk in Frankenmuth, Michigan, a rural German community, in 1938. Even then it was not devoured by scholars, only scrutinized in 1969. The insights gained, relatively recently, have put to rest any credible doubts concerning the reality of Bach's faith. In the markings there are four comments in Bach's hand that directly relate music to worship. He even filled in some of Luther's commentary that was missing from the *Calov* Bible, demonstrating his familiarity with and careful study of Luther's writings and of course the Bible itself.

Bach also marked, some with unusual emphasis, eight passages of commentary having to do with one's office and calling. Christoph Trautmann wrote that Bach's Bible marginalia and such evidence of earnest study of the Word "reveal the conviction of Bach, the Lutheran cantor, that his office claimed the whole man and the whole artist as one indivisible unit" and that they "must be taken seriously as the expression of a mature person conscious of his responsibility, as a Christian and an artist."[8]

Of Bach's four major biographers since his death, two of them—Nikolaus Forkel and Philipp Spitta—strongly emphasized the nationalistic aspect of Bach's work and legacy, the constant consciousness of German art. Albert Schweitzer, who was a noted theologian as well as a master church organist, stressed Bach's spiritual side in his mammoth biography of one hundred years ago, discerning a certain mysticism therein. Bach biographer Christoph Wolff, in our day, has focused on Bach the composer and musician, more than Bach the nationalistic or religious figure. In fact, though Bach's attitudes and church work are much discussed, Wolff titled the chapter about Bach's beliefs "Metaphysics," not "Christianity" or "Spirituality."

Regarding how his Christian music was received by contemporaries—or indeed by history—Bach was writing for an audience of one: God. In the providence of passing time, Luther and Bach both would be surprised to hear their music—especially *"Ein Feste Burg"* ("A Mighty Fortress"), Luther's martial anthem upon which Bach wrote several variations—sung in Roman Catholic churches today. Such factors reinforce a characterization of Johann Sebastian Bach as "the last of the old, the first of the new."

3

THE GRAND TOUR

It was my intention to advance the music in the divine service toward its very end and purpose, a regulated church music in honor of God. . . . So God willed to bring about an opportunity that will not only put me in a better position as far as the subsistence of my livelihood is concerned, but will also make it possible for me . . . to persevere in working for my very end, which consists in organizing church music well.

—Johann Sebastian Bach

Just as we cannot understand the music of Bach apart from his faith, neither can we understand the life of Bach without visiting his family.[1] (Note to the reader: You will find a list of Bach's family members in Appendix B.) It was in the late 1500s that Veit (Vitus) Bach, a "baker of white bread," settled in Wechmar of Thuringia. He evidently moved from Pressburg, Hungary (later the birthplace of Johann Nepomuk Hummel, a student of Mozart and a neglected genius of the late Classical period), known now as Bratislava. Yet Albert Schweitzer's research suggested that Veit Bach merely returned to Thuringia, whence the family originated, because of anti-Lutheran and anti-German persecution in Hungarian lands during the Counter-Reformation.[2] In Germany, Veit then lived for a time in Ohrdruf, a little town built around a chapel and monastery dating back to 727—a Benedictine settlement founded by Irish missionaries, likely including St. Boniface. Some of the first missionaries, including St. Columbanus, who planted seeds of Christianity on German soil, were Irish.[3]

Johann Sebastian Bach was vitally interested in his ancestry and compiled a genealogy in 1735. According to family legend, Veit "found the greatest pleasure playing a little cittern," an instrument of the guitar family whose name's similarity to "sitar" and "zither" suggests its characteristics. Veit's son Johannes ("Hans," who died in 1626) turned an avocation into a profession when he became a piper, nicknamed *der Spielmann*, "the player," and the Bachs were off to the races, or to the music fests. In all, fifty-three musical Bachs are on the family tree. By the way, if it seems that every Tom, Dick, and Harry in the Bach family seemed to bear the Christian name of Johann, it is because that was virtually the case. The use of Johann as a first name for every son is a longstanding tradition, extending even into the early twentieth century. In most cases it was not the name of common address. Family and friends invariably addressed the principal subject of this biography as "Sebastian."

The father of Johann Sebastian was Johann Ambrosius. As noted, he was a *Stadtpfeiffer*, an official town musician, court trumpter, and freelance musician. His cousins Johann Michael and Johann Christoph were remarkable composers in nearby towns, noted masters of composition and musical innovations. Bach's mother, Elizabeth, also was descended from a musical family. Ambrosius had a twin brother, another Johann Christoph, who was similar in more than musical talent. The brothers were so alike that their own wives could not tell them apart. When one fell ill the other consistently did likewise, and they died within days of each other.

Ambrosius and Elizabeth died when Johann Sebastian, their eighth child, was nine years old. He and his brother Johann Jacob were taken to the household of their eldest brother Johann Christoph, a church organist, in nearby Ohrdruf, the ancestral home of the Bach family's musical progenitor, Veit Bach. Bach scarcely knew his brother Christoph, who was fifteen years his senior and had left home early to study with Johann Pachelbel—a family friend and godfather to Bach's sister Johanna Juditha. Pachelbel was organist at Johann Christoph's wedding ceremony. (Pachelbel composed the famous *Canon*, so familiar today and often played as wedding music.)

Bach likely received his earliest training in composition

and keyboard in the household of his brother. Here arose two stories that might be only legend, but their flavor confirms his musical affinity. In one story, young Bach was forbidden access to a musical score from which he wished to play. He discovered that the cabinet where it was locked away had a lattice door with openings allowing a boy's hand to slip through. Every night while the house slept, young Sebastian quietly secured the musical manuscript and copied it by moonlight. When almost completed, however, the elder brother discovered the game and destroyed the copy as punishment for disobedience. This story led some people to conclude that the eyestrain resulted in Bach's blindness at the end of his life.

Another story also concerned possible friction between the brothers. In this legend the pair argued at bedtime and Bach went to the keyboard and played an "unresolved chord," a dissonance that universally leaves listeners' ears uncomfortable, driving Christoph to distraction when he heard it. He had to rush downstairs and play that last chord before he could sleep. A later legend claims that Constanze Mozart played an unresolved chord when all other methods failed to rouse her husband Wolfgang Amadeus from bed in the morning.

Despite these accounts, which might be what we call urban legends today, young Bach received his first serious, and evidently intense, musical training from his elder brother. The youngster absorbed keyboard instruction on both harpsichord and organ, which have very different dynamics. Eisenach, little Eisenach, also had one of the grandest organs in Europe, so it is doubtless the case that Sebastian was already preconditioned—by listening to its regal sound and witnessing the intricacies of its mechanisms—to master the "king of instruments."[4] It is also likely that Bach began his lifelong affection for playing the lute in Christoph's household.

Bach reportedly began composing his first music—variations on Pachelbel's music—at the age of ten, the same as did another young music lover, born the same year as Bach in nearby Halle: Georg Friedrich Händel. Bach's precocity was evident from the start. His compositions were not mere variations but extensions, different structural forms, new harmonies, unconventional cadences and endings[5] based on Pachelbel's tunes.

After five years the household was not able to support the fifteen-year-old. Christoph secured a position for his brother in the choir of St. Michael's Church in Lüneburg. Bach and a friend, Georg Erdmann, walked north to Lüneburg, closer to Hamburg where the famous composer Georg Phillip Telemann reigned, and where the venerable organist Johann Adam Reincken played the mighty St. Catherine Church organ; and closer to the court at Celle, where French musicians were imported (Duke Georg Wilhelm's wife was a French Huguenot). He also found himself near Lübeck, the center of the north German school of organ playing, where Bach listened to its exemplar, Dietrich Buxtehude, and is believed to have received instruction from him.

The scholastic—nonmusical—aspect of Bach's education, in classroom and on his own in the libraries, was not insignificant. Under German-Lutheran law, families could receive punishment if children (boys *and* girls) between the ages of five and twelve were not educated in school. The lower grades were called "German School" and taught religion (the Bible, the hymn-books, catechism), grammar, and arithmetic. The higher grades were called "Latin" because instruction in that language was added to the advanced lessons.[6] It is reported that Bach was always at the head of his classes, often advanced as many as four years over his classmates.[7]

Bach's Lüneburg schooling—principally Christian theology and Latin, Greek, and French—was provided in exchange for singing in the St. Michael's choir. He was reputed to have had a beautiful soprano voice, which soon cracked as he matured. He remained in the program, however, thanks to his proficiency on various instruments. And, while he could, he betook himself to absorb everything possible in the church's musical library—one of the finest in Europe, built upon the archives of the church's first Lutheran cantor, Friedrich Emanuel Praetorius—of more than eleven hundred musical manuscripts by approximately 175 composers.

Praetorius possibly was a descendant of the important figure in German High-Renaissance music, Michael Praetorius, a *Kapellmeister* of the Lüneburg court and known today as the composer of the *Dances of Terpsichore*, merry dances oft recorded. Michael had also compiled the enormous collection of scores and theory, *Syntama Musicum*. Without the archival work of these two men, we would know much less about seventeenth-century German and European music. Bach, for his part, learned much from their work.

Bach frequently walked to Hamburg to listen to the aged organist Reincken, a disciple of the distinguished Dutch composer Jan Pieterszoon van Sweelinck, who exemplified yet another "school" of organ playing and composition, particularly the art of variations. Sweelinck was the composer of the haunting "My Young Life Has an End." God surely orchestrated these opportunities for Bach to learn his future trade and fulfill his talents.

During one of his walks, returning to Lüneburg from Hamburg, approximately thirty miles, an event occurred—another urban (or "rural") legend?—without which, Albert Schweitzer wrote, "no biography of Bach is complete." So we dutifully shall tell it. "Once on the way back from Hamburg to Lüneburg, Bach, hungry and penniless, was standing in front of an inn. The windows opened, and some herring-heads were thrown into the street. He picked them up and found in each of them a Danish ducat. This anecdote . . . is told by Marpurg in his *Legenden einziger Musikheiligen*, Cologne, 1786."[8]

Within three years Bach was accomplished enough on the organ to accept a post in his native Thuringia region, at the "New Church" of Arnstadt, where one of his grandfathers had lived. Family connections might have affected his selection, however, it was the eighteen-year-old's prowess on the new organ that seemed to impress Arnstadt. Reportedly, he was merely testing their organ as a renowned amateur, and when they heard the young man play, they offered him a job.

Things were in store for the young musician. Bach was ready to pull out all the stops. The metaphor refers to organ playing, but in Bach's case, it literally was the case.

STARTING WORK

At eighteen years old, Bach was hired as the organist in Arnstadt. A new job, at the "New Church." Not the grandest organ in north Germany, but the newest; and it absorbed his attention. It was an honor to his talent that he was not required to perform many other duties than to play during services, accompany congregational hymns, and improvise chorales to introduce portions of the liturgy.

The orders of the Lutheran service, by Bach's time, reflected the points of Lutheran theology as well as the nationalistic concerns of a people's church, but they were not radically different from the Catholic Mass. Luther's revolutionary changes did not extend much into the form, or format, of the worship service. In fact, the Mass was not banished, but, shorn of the Catholics' observance of sacrifice, which was replaced by the sermon. Therefore the Lutherans retained the great choral constituents of musical worship (the kyrie, Gloria, Credo, Sanctus with Benedictus, and Agnus Dei) and in the same places in the service. Music from Catholic—even Italian Catholic—Masses routinely was performed in German Lutheran churches and included in printed hymnbooks. These changes serve to illustrate the evolving emphases and diminished antagonisms of the two branches of European Christianity.

As the sermon took on more of a role in Lutheran services, the hymns and music reflected the character of each Sunday's theological focus. Hence the Gradual, between the epistle and the gospel reading, became an important element in the presentation of the entire service's theme. The choir and the congregation could both be involved. They and the musicians were aware of this significant role, and so were composers.

There were new uses for the texts; new need for spiritual poems; a new burden—or opportunity—to provide a fresh exposition of the day's message. In the process, the mechanical, ritual, statutory portions of the old service receded.[9]

At the beginning of Bach's career he was so devoted to the organ that when it was suggested that he lend a hand, perhaps with the choir direction or by occasionally teaching extra classes, Bach refused. Composing was soon to come, but at first he practically lived with the "king of instruments," all the time learning its sonorities and possibilities, and experimenting.

Even when Bach allowed himself time for romance, it was in the shadow of the church organ. It was reported that he brought a young woman to the choir's balcony and he was reprimanded. Bach claimed that he was instructing the girl (a distant cousin, Maria Barbara, whom he was to marry) in music.

There are other reports of friction during his service at Arnstadt. He was once attacked on the street by a music student who resented Bach's insulting assessment of his abilities. The student wielded a club and Bach drew a knife in self-defense before they were separated. When called before the consistory to defend himself in the matter of the scuffle, Bach merely repeated his opinion. Whether Bach's appraisal was justified or not, again he was admonished. Bach's resentment of occasional teaching assignments that took him away from the organ was compounded by the awkward situation of being younger than many of his pupils.

In 1705, two years into his employment, he asked permission to travel to Lübeck in order to listen again to the influential organist Buxtehude. He was granted four weeks but returned after four months. Mesmerized by the mighty organ and the performances of the north German / Danish style of church organ music, Bach attended every service. He evidently established a relationship with the legendary Buxtehude and learned all he could. When he returned to Arnstadt, he calmly responded to his consistory's displeasure by reminding them that he had left his duties in the good hands of one whom he trusted, who happened to be another Bach cousin. Beginning with his first service after returning, he played different styles of organ chorales, to the confusion and consternation of the committee.

Chorales were an important aspect of the Lutheran service. To radically reduce the definition of the chorale, it is a brief strain of music, usually familiar to worshipers and "borrowed" from a hymn or other music. It can stand alone, but its main function is as a musical interlude or introduction to parts of the service (liturgy, readings, sermon, offering, etc.); therefore it is often paired with the word *prelude*. The chorale can be an organ solo, other instrumental, vocal ensemble, or any combination.

From the twenty-first century, we can look back and see that the chorale filled in the cracks of services where music already predominated. Part of a three- or four-hour worship service was a glorious wall-to-wall sensory experience, and the chorale provided segues at appropriate moments. To grasp for a common parallel, we can say they were tunes or jingles—like contemporary media commercials, they were short, accessible, and familiar to their audience.

Traditional phrases from familiar hymns and liturgy were meant to be improvised before portions of the service. Embellishments were essential to the variety program that was the Lutheran service of the day. They glorified God in their technical display and provided "intermissions" during church services that could last several hours. Therefore an organist's improvisational talent was important. But Bach, on his return from Lübeck, praised God in a new way that worshipers in Arnstadt had never heard in organ chorales: grand, multilayered, lengthy; variations, trills, familiar hymns played in new ways, stated and mirrored, sounds produced by unorthodox combinations of organ-stops; bass notes—no, actual counterpoint-melodies—produced by Bach's feet virtually dancing over the foot pedals. Bach's son C.P.E. later described his father the organist: "With his two feet he could perform . . . passages which would be enough to provoke many a skilled clavier player with five fingers."

In all of this he fulfilled the experiments of local masters Johann Pachelbel and uncles Johann Christoph and Michael. And he extended the style of the revered Buxtehude. Bach, his hands and feet flying across the multikeyboard organ, left his listeners (or at least his music committee) somewhat impressed but very confused. There were more scoldings.

≈

All of these factors resulted in Bach's departure from Arnstadt. In 1707 he accepted a post as organist in Mühlhausen's St. Blasius

Church and bequeathed his post as Arnstadt's organist to his cousin Ernst Bach, the son of his father's twin brother. Bach's annual salary at St. Blasius was 85 gulden (approximately $6,000 in today's value), "three coombs of grain" (approximately 750 pounds), two cords of wood, six trusses of brushwood, and three pounds of fish, all to be delivered to his door.[10]

His duties were somewhat expanded to require more composition. Larger-scale organ works were performed at this church, even "secular" pieces like his stunning *Toccata and Fugue in D minor*. Bach always regarded every piece of his music as unto the Lord, but the cantata was a specific genre of church music he first addressed during his short Mühlhausen year (the facilities were compromised after a major fire decimated the church and organ). Its name derived from the Latin root word for *sing*, the church cantata was more dedicated to function than form. The cantata employed, usually, a full choir and soloists, organist and instruments, solo players and ensembles. Sometimes movements were broken up and performed throughout the service, serving to introduce readings, echo themes of the season or the sermon message, and facilitate contemplation. Otherwise they served as a solid "second sermon" on the text for the day. Cantatas did not replace any part of the Lutheran service but added to it in a variety of ways. As Bach made the cantata a musical and worship *experience*, church services became magnets that attracted and inspired awestruck worshipers.

It was Bach who took the form and codified its elements so definitively that no composers after him altered it further.

Today cantatas are usually performed in a concert hall, outside spiritual settings, or in recordings, an unfortunate tendency of contemporary culture to transform music and art of the church, once so full of vitality, to abstractions.

The postings in Arnstadt and Mühlhausen were brief but nevertheless overflowed with music, astonishing in its quality and quantity. Bach's devotion to the music of the church honored traditions going back to Luther, but also—odd as it might seem to today's ears—was regarded as revolutionary. As always, the gospel was at the center of his music. He built all his church music—which included not just chorales and cantatas but also motets, hymns, and eventually Masses, oratorios, and Passions—on words from Scripture, praising God and evangelizing listeners. If another purpose was to fulfill his talents and create beautiful music, that, too, Bach recognized as ultimately honoring God.

During Bach's short tenure at Mühlhausen, tension between Lutherans and Pietists was rife. Pietists denounced "wordly" music and extravagent worship. Yet the Pietist-leaning Blasiuskirche nevertheless employed Bach, who evidently experienced few strictures. He continued to compose and perform as he had previously, and the minister of the rival Lutheran church even served as godfather to one of the Bachs' sons. In a society still inclined to dispute every minor point of Bible doctrine, Bach likely survived this and other similar challenges because he forthrightly adhered to Scripture and Scripture alone, with no shadow of turning in his work. He evidently impressed sectarian factions as being above the disputes, loyal to the Word of God alone.

However easily Bach navigated the churning waters of theological disputes, the fire that devastated Mühlhausen made it easier for him to move on. Bach had received an offer of tremendous honor and prestige as court organist, concertmaster, and chief chamber musician at the court of Duke Wilhelm Ernst of Sachsen-Weimar. This royal appointment allowed for both Christian and secular music to be composed and performed, and provided Bach with helpers—at last, more than a solitary bellows blower for the organ. In 1708 he assumed his duties in Weimar, actually his second "tour" there. In 1703 he had served as a musician and court "lackey" (the actual title!) for a few months.

Instead of contending with church councils, consistories, and clergy, and sometimes relying on freelance fees from funerals and weddings, Bach now was in a professional environment where music was appreciated—including music from afar, for the duke's nephew, Prince Wilhelm Ernst, was an avid student and in particular a devotee of the Italian style. One reason for Bach's hire was to propagate the new forms of concert music sweeping Europe. There would be twenty members of the court band under his direction.

Although some church composing and performing were components of his duties in Weimar, Bach could easily have chosen to forsake church music, to climb the ladder to the glittering worlds of courts and concert halls. But God's music remained central to him. At Weimar he was to write at least one cantata every month—a stupendous achievement, even without his other output. And there was a creative explosion of new forms of composition (stylistic hallmarks of Italian opera entered Bach's cantatas, for instance); of categories (Bach composed concert and chamber music, including the famed *Brandenburg Concertos*, at Weimar); and experimentation with new instruments, including clavichord, harpsichord, solo violin, lute, and flute.

As he had earlier incorporated some French, Danish, and Dutch styles when given opportunities, Bach feasted upon Italian fare at the Weimar court. The prince had acquired many musical scores by Antonio Vivaldi, the "Red-Haired Priest of Venice," who had composed hundreds of concerti and established the basic elements thereof—solo instrument(s) contrasted with a chamber ensemble or orchestra; three fast-slow-fast movements; encouragement of performers' embellishments; and showcase cadenzas (improvisation by soloists near the ends of movements). Vivaldi led the orchestra at a school for "wayward women," and his diverse catalog of compositions reflects the particular instruments mastered by soloists who passed through. He wrote more than five hundred concertos—or, in the common joke of detractors, he composed one concerto five hundred times. But Bach was clearly impressed and mightily influenced by Vivaldi's technical style. He transcribed some of Vivaldi's works, sometimes rearranging instrumentation and keys or adjusting structure, preserving melodies but always making them his own. From the Italians he came to appreciate *cantabile* elements: sweet melodies, not all "structure."

Bach wrote his own harpsichord concertos for two, three, and four harpsichords. And he wrote concertos for other solo instruments, or combinations of solo instruments, all the while exploring the dynamics of concert music. In his compositions, soloists sometimes contrasted with the ensemble, sometimes integrated themselves. They were allowed to improvise and embellish. Sometimes they carried a lead melody only to pass it off to the ensemble and then seize it again. After a century of European experimentation, Bach transformed the concerto into a heartier and more codified form. It was bequeathed to Classical era composers who followed him, principally Haydn and Beethoven and especially Mozart. (It should be noted that Bach's contemporary Georg Friedrich Händel expanded the orchestral scope, if not the actual form, when he composed his *Concerti Grossi*—grand concertos.)

Bach cannot be termed one of musical history's "late bloomers," since he was very good at his craft at such an early age. Yet his steady path to greatness saw an uptick during his service in Weimar. His performances were welcomed in other churches, not just in the court chapel, and his secular works were performed at salons, in public houses, in gardens, and in concert halls. His fame was spreading. He was called upon to test instruments and to consult in the design and repair of organs. When composers and musicians traveled anywhere near Saxony, many endeavored to visit Bach, discuss music, and hear him play.

Bach was to father twenty children, and almost symbolic of his fecundity during the Weimar years, two sons born there—Wilhelm Friedemann (1710) and Carl Philipp Emanuel (1714)—went on to become distinguished and famous composers themselves.

It might be hard to believe today, but some clerics and consistories criticized Bach's music for being too "light" and "theatrical," not just too "complicated," which was the more frequent complaint. In all cases, Bach responded that music was to honor the Lord, and anything that bespoke the compromise of the highest standards was unacceptable. Yet complaints and bureaucratic friction perhaps made it inevitable that Bach would clash with the authorities at the court of Sachsen-Gotha as he had done in the churches of Arnstadt and Mühlhausen. Although Bach did not violate his contract, the court, perhaps out of jealousy, attempted to restrict his freelance composing and performing in public and, occasionally, at rival courts. In 1716, a man whose abilities Bach considered inferior to his own was hired over his objections. There were many such clashes. All of those incidents made it easy for Bach not just to scan the horizon for any new position, but to seek for himself a position with authority: *Kapellmeister*. English speakers often assume this title appertains to a religious chapel, but an orchestra is also a *Kapelle*. (A dance ensemble is called *Tanzkapelle*, a military band is a *Militärkapelle*, and so forth; music without instruments is *a cappella*.) The *Kapellmeister* is the master or conductor of a chamber orchestra.

≈

There was an opening for a *Kapellmeister* in Cöthen, under Prince Leopold von Anhalt-Cöthen, and the court was very happy to have someone of Bach's prestige and talents. Bach received the invitation to the appointment; he accepted. But when he announced his intentions to his employer in Weimar, Duke Wilhelm-Ernst of Sachsen-Gotha, Bach promptly was tossed into jail. For a month in 1717, he lived behind bars as the Ducal court tried all means—mostly relying on a waiting game—to dissuade the composer from taking up the new position. The Saxon duke blinked first, and Bach was declared free to move to his next post.

Thus ended Bach's time in Weimar, a spurt of some of music history's most remarkable creativity, possibly overshadowed only by Bach's activity at this *next* posting.

Prince Leopold of Cöthen was only twenty-three, but—surely the personification of an enlightened monarch—he loved music with all his soul. In spite of the title *Kapellmeister*, Bach technically was the personal composer to the prince and in practical terms was free to do as he pleased as composer and performer.

Posterity should be grateful that the prince recognized no little anomaly in his sanction of music, for his was a Calvinist court. His mother was the austere stereotype who disapproved of music and "entertainment," and in a few years the prince's new wife was destined to be an even more effective spoilsport. We are reminded of an assessment by Theodore Roosevelt, himself (Dutch) Reformed, who wrote that a regrettable aspect of the Puritan version of Calvinism was its "tendency to confuse pleasure and vice." By the music-loving prince's compromise solution, Bach was to write scant music for the court's church but was free and encouraged to compose, conduct, and perform for concerts and recitals. Fully one-fourth of the prince's court budget during Bach's time in his service was expended on music—instruction, staffing, staging, and performing. Besides luring Bach with a handsome salary, Leopold generously paid musicians from other principalities to join his musical corps. The prince himself was an enthusiastic musician and frequently played viola da gamba, violin, or harpsichord in performances.

Coaxing the ascendant personality Johann Sebastian Bach to his court undoubtedly pleased Prince Leopold greatly. For Bach, the freedom he enjoyed and the musicians at his disposal surely approximated a musician's paradise. During five short years Bach produced a freshet of astounding works, including completing the six memorable Brandenburg concertos begun in Weimar; the *Well-Tempered Clavier* (Book One), which became a standard component of music theory and the performance repertoire; the suites for violoncello; the French and English suites for harpsichord; the suites for lute; sonatas and partitas for solo violin; and many other solo and chamber masterpieces.

Bach and his prince became personal friends. They often traveled to other cities to attend concerts and recitals. Returning from one such trip in 1720, Bach learned that his wife, Maria Barbara, had fallen ill, died, and was buried during his absence. Bach, then thirty-five, was devastated; theirs had been a happy marriage, and four children were now his to rear alone.

≈

After five years at the court in Cöthen, despite Bach's freedom and comforts, he grew restive. Plainly, he missed the church duties—liturgical music, organ playing, organizing services, teaching—he had enjoyed in previous posts. Without a doubt, he longed to write music again for Lutheran worship. Perhaps he desired a larger platform than the small principality of Anhalt-Cöthen. He inquired about openings in the big cities of Hamburg (organist), Berlin (*Kapellmeister*), and Leipzig (cantor). Again, English speakers can be thrown off by the word *cantor*'s similarity to a singer, one who chants, or the vocalist in a synagogue. In German ecclesiastical tradition, the cantor was the director of all music programs; in a scholastic setting, akin to a dean of music.

At Hamburg he was declined, but for economic, not artistic, reasons. The story is a colorful attestation of the high regard that some officials had for Bach:

> It so happened that the organist's post at St. Jacob's church became vacant in September 1720 . . . A few weeks afterwards, Bach went to Hamburg and performed on the organ of St. Catharine's church before Reincken, who was then nearly a hundred years old, and a select company. The story is well known of how the old master of the organ went up to the younger one, who had just improvised for half an hour on the chorale *An Wasserflüssen Babylon*, and complimented him with the words: "I thought this art had perished, but I see that it still lives on in you." The praise was even more flattering inasmuch as Reincken himself had treated the same melody at length in a chorale prelude, of which he was not a little proud.

> Bach was exempted from giving a trial exhibition for the post at St. Jacob's. We may be sure that Neumeister, who was

the clergyman of the church, strenuously urged his election. His candidature failed, however. The choice, which was made on the 19th December, fell on a certain Johann Joachim Heitmann. The church accounts let us see wherein consisted his superiority over Bach in the eyes of the authorities of St. Jacob's. On 6 January 1721, he paid into the church treasury the sum of 4000 Marks in acknowledgment of his election. The fact that he expended so much to secure the post leads us to surmise that it must have had some very lucrative perquisites attached to it.

Neumeister was indignant, and gave vent to his vexation in a sermon. Speaking at Christmas of the angels who made music at the birth of Christ, he added that their art would certainly have availed them nothing in Hamburg; he really believed, he said, that if one of the angels of Bethlehem, who could play divinely, were to come down from heaven and try to become organist at St. Jacob's, but had no money, he would simply have to fly back again.[11]

Such setbacks coincided with Prince Leopold's marriage to the stern Princess Friederika Henrietta von Anhalt-Bernburg, as noted. The evidently pliant husband likewise cooled his passion for music making. Timing was in Bach's favor, however. Soon after he was offered and left for the post of cantor at Leipzig, the young prince died unexpectedly. There was music at his funeral, and Bach returned to compose and lead it.

Within a year of his wife Maria Barbara's death, Bach remarried. The twenty-year-old Anna Magdalena Wülcken, seventeen years his junior, proved to be another match made in heaven. A gifted soprano who performed at the court in Cöthen, she was the daughter of a noted trumpeter, and she provided all the professional support and household leadership of Bach's first wife, Barbara—which by all accounts was substantial and an inspiration to friends and family—and was also a mature partner to Bach the music maker. She continued to sing outside the home at concerts and gatherings. She played several instruments well, including the keyboard, and frequently transcribed or copied her husband's scores as needed. For her instruction, and as a token of his love and respect, Bach was to compose a series of keyboard pieces known as "The Notebook for Anna Magdalena Bach," today a part of the standard keyboard repertoire.

In 1723 the Bachs moved to Leipzig, the largest city yet where Bach received a commission. With all of its allure, Bach had no way of knowing whether it would be just another way-station in his career of Christian service and music.

4

THE MAN
WHO TRANSCRIBED
GOD'S MUSIC

I needed to be industrious. Anyone who does
likewise can come just as far.

—Johann Sebastian Bach

L eipzig was to be Bach's last earthly posting. For
twenty-seven years the city was to be his home and
his platform. His initial appointment was as cantor
(chiefly, choir director) of St. Thomas Church, but his duties
were expanded to many functions at three other churches as well
as other venues in the city. On paper, the move was a backward
step. At Cöthen, Bach had enjoyed freedom and authority as a

Kapellmeister. In his new post, he was a cantor, obliged again to teach, manage, and be subordinate to school officials. Classes were not all music; he also oversaw Latin instruction. He actually was subject to two sets of bosses, the church consistory and the town officials in charge of events. They often clashed with each other and Bach, inevitably, was to clash with each of them. He held choir practices on Mondays, Tuesdays, Wednesdays, and Fridays. On Saturdays there were rehearsals for choir, soloists, and orchestra for the next day's cantata service. *This* was an alluring job?

But Leipzig became Bach's virtual music box! He accepted more and more of his duties with joy, tempered only by frustrations over the usual bureaucratic friction and occasional lack of resources. For instance, at one time an organist named Görner was appointed at St. Thomas over Bach's wishes. In one moment of frustration, Bach railed at Görner's playing, threw his wig at him, and called him "no better than a cobbler!" Nevertheless, these were fleeting moments, as were his tiffs with councils; in fact, Görner eventually was invited to be guardian of the Bach children.

Overall, in Leipzig's employment Bach enjoyed a great opportunity to spread his wings. The four churches—St. Thomas, St. Nicholas, St. Peter, and the city's own "New Church"—offered a range of quality organs and a variety of attractive acoustical aspects. The most minor aspect of an organ's sound, and the particular qualities of a sanctuary or hall, always meant as much to Bach as to any composer who ever made music. In Leipzig he had more resources than at any previous job; the large city provided singers and musicians in great numbers. The wealth of city, church, and school—St. Thomas School was renowned far and wide for its quality of staff—assured support for major religious observances and musical events. Bach, at the center of all this, saw his prestige, and therefore his effective service, increase greatly.

A torrent of creativity flowed in Leipzig with a force and consistency that seems scarcely human. To his composing and performing, administrative duties and teaching, Bach added other work: freelance consultant to instrument makers, salesman of musical scores, composer for private functions like weddings and funerals, private teacher to a generation of eminent composers and players, and director of the Collegium Musicum. Founded in 1702 by the esteemed Georg Philipp Telemann, the Collegium was a private association, a club of sorts, which met weekly in Zimmermann's Coffee Shop. Every Friday evening there were public performances—many written by Bach, often performed by Bach—of solo music, ensemble pieces, songs, motets, and other music, secular and religious; and of short mini-operas, generally called "secular cantatas."

As cantor of St. Thomas in Leipzig, Bach was a *de facto* director of music in the church, and dean of music in the St. Thomas school. Religious and civic authorities heralded the appointment. The duties, even as they evolved over nearly three decades, were heavy with responsibility. Bach's reputation was such that he should have been obliged to work under fewer strictures than in previous jobs in smaller cities. One might expect fewer "mundane" tasks like classroom instruction.

Some historians have asserted that Bach's assignment list and the bureaucrats looking over his shoulder were demeaning. As Schweitzer noted, however, Bach's duties were numerous but not especially onerous.[1] The title *cantor* was a word that covered a multitude of dins, as noted, and eventually he devolved some duties, for instance Latin instruction, to subordinates. And when all was said and done, "the Cantor had the second position within the pecking order of [St. Thomas's entire] ministry."[2]

Never abandoning his prime assignments, he nevertheless became something of a production manager of the musical worship at Leipzig's churches, as well as overseer of the civic musical celebrations. Schweitzer even observed wryly that Bach was able to play two intrusive bodies, the civil council and the church consistory, against each other, to his ultimate freedom of action.

Nevertheless, on paper—literally, by terms of his contract—Bach was, at first, treated peremptorily. Permission of the *Bürgermeister* was required when Bach traveled outside Leipzig. For the sake of economy, the overseeing of routine instrumental practice was added to vocal training of students. His presence was required when boys' choirs accompanied funeral processions. And as a final step before his hiring, Bach "had to undergo, as was the custom of the time, an examination of his religious belief, out of which he came satisfactorily. He also had to sign the [Lutheran] Concordia Formula, for without signing this no one could hold an appointment in Saxony."[3]

The Formula of Concord was an edict delivered by the Elector of Saxony in 1580, a confession intended definitively to particularize the differences from the Roman Church, condemn liberal Lutheran tendencies, oppose Calvinism, and unite the Lutheran factions. It addressed original sin, free will, the Lord's Supper, predestination, the rule of faith and the creed, justification, good works, the Law and the gospel, the third use of the Law, the person of Christ, the descent of Christ into hell, and customs of the church. It was approved at first by eighty-six of the German states and eventually became, in almost creedal fashion, the handbook of Lutheran orthodoxy. As stated, Bach passed the examination concerning the Formula of Concord, undoubtedly in happy affirmation to boot.

In all, however, numerous routine duties did not overwhelm Bach's schedule. His staff enlarged until he was able to delegate chores (unless he needed the freelance fees), and sometimes he became confident enough—of his performers' abilities or his own security—to be lax in convening classes or holding rehearsals. Almost alone among Bach's biographers, Schweitzer maintains that Bach enjoyed an amicable relationship and a rather freedom-filled schedule in Leipzig.[4]

At St. Thomas, Bach was given "freedom" from organ playing. St. Thomas had an organist, whom Bach supervised, and so a phase of astonishing composition and virtuosity, perhaps without parallel in cultural history, came to an end. Of course, Bach did not abandon the "king of instruments," but his requisite duties and preoccupations shifted elsewhere.[5]

~

Despite the stated Lutheran orthodoxy of St. Thomas, all

churches in the region felt the creeping influence of Calvinism and Pietism, sects that discouraged music and joyful forms of worship. The "concert style" of church music (for example, Bach's use of chorales, sinfonias, anthems, and performances within a service) disappeared from many Lutheran services in the generation after Bach, "and the town choirs that had been allotted to the churches ceased to exist. . . . [C]ongregational singing became the characteristic and sole service-music of the Protestant church. In the epoch of rationalism and pietism the ideal was realised. . . . However barbarously rationalism behaved towards the old hymn, it did good work for congregational singing."[6]

Because Bach refused to abandon the musical forms that had evolved in Germany and over which he exercised such mastery, ambiguity sometimes surrounded him. He could be revolutionary, yet he "spoke" through motets and cantatas and fugues. "Old fashioned!" Therefore he was on a collision course with a religion that showed signs of abandoning the grand architecture of worship and with a society and art that was about to turn light and "airy" for a generation. If he sensed the impending changes, he evidently cared little. Certainly he did not tailor his music—neither playing nor composing—to new trends.

Overall, day-to-day at St. Thomas he was to be a church employee in the fullest sense, serving in many capacities. In matters of theology he was a follower, not a leader. He taught catechism classes, true enough, but otherwise was a lifelong student of the Bible and of Lutheran doctrine. His musical breakthroughs were revolutionary, but as a Christian exegete he was an evangelist, not a theologian; he was a servant.

Comparisons between Luther and Bach are tempting and valid. But the most obvious link is that Luther was a theologian who loved music and used it in ministry. Bach was a musician who loved doctrine and its propagation through his art. When the organ was his chief instrument, it vividly symbolized the homogeneous faith life of those times: a mighty instrument with hundreds of performance options and countless sounds, it was played by one performer who drew all of its elements into unity. Unlike the Romantic era over the musical horizon, the Baroque (particularly the organ music of Bach) represented a dedication to sublimate self, to be synonymous with praise, to embrace the complex and, yes, the scientific.

Bach's "patron saint" Martin Luther had said, "A good schoolmaster must also be a musician; otherwise I would not look at him as an educator." Music historian Paul Nettl defined that point of view in this way: music was considered a matter not of entertainment but of edification and education. "This educational philosophy of music goes back to a time when music, astronomy, arithmetic and geometry built the 'quadrivium' of medieval education. Whereas modern man listens to church music as a kind of emotional accompaniment, music in Bach's time (thanks largely to Luther) was an actual working part of the service."[7]

A window to Bach's preoccupations and his duties, as well as an understanding of how church services have changed over three centuries, can be gleaned from a run-through of the requirements at Leipzig's four churches.[8]

Cantatas were sung each Sunday, with the exception of

the last three Sundays in Advent and the six of Lent. In addition there were the three Feasts of the Virgin, the New Year, Epiphany, Ascension, the Feast of St. John, Michaelmas (St. Michael and All Angels), and the Reformation Feast—in all, fifty-nine cantatas every year.

The service in the city's two main churches began at seven o'clock in the morning. The organ prelude was followed by the motet; then came the introit; after this the kyrie, which was sung once in German, in the hymn "*Kyrie, Gott Vater in Ewigkeit*" ("Kyrie, God Father in Heav'n above"), and once in Latin. The Gloria was intoned from the altar and answered either by the choir with *et in terra pax* or by the congregation with "*Allein Gott in der Höh' sei Ehr*" ("To God Alone on High Be Praise"), the German version of the Gloria. After the collect, the epistle was sung from the old psalmody. This was followed by a congregational hymn, after which the pastor chanted the gospel reading.

It was only during Bach's tenure that the organ regularly accompanied the congregational hymn singing; previously it was *a cappella*, or stanzas alternated between choir and organ (partly to keep singers in tune).[9] Then the pastor intoned the Credo, the most solemn part of the liturgy, and the organist began a prelude, keeping mainly in the keys that the instruments needed for tuning as they prepared. At a sign from the cantor, the organist ceased and the cantata began, at the end of which the hymn "*Wir glauben all an einen Gott*" ("We all Believe in One True God; Maker") was sung. The cantata lasted an average of twenty minutes.

In the summer the cantor did not need to keep to this time so precisely as in the winter, when the cold church hastened things along (services generally lasted three or four hours). In St. Nicholas's Church the choristers maintained a coal fire; at St. Thomas they left the sanctuary during the sermon and warmed themselves in the school. They did not, however, escape the sermon. While in retreat at the warm schoolroom, they were obliged to read the printed message under the watchful eye of the rector. There was no fear of their miscalculating the time, since the sermon, according to rule, had to last exactly an hour, from eight o'clock to nine o'clock.

A prayer and the blessing followed the sermon, and then a congregational hymn led into the second part of the service, the Communion celebration. German hymns were usually sung during the Communion. The choir at St. Thomas was as a rule no longer at its full strength at this stage of the service, as the alumni had to prepare the table in the school for the meal at eleven o'clock. Bach played the organ during the Communion, with plenty of opportunity for improvisation, suggested by his many chorale preludes upon Communion hymns.

At a quarter to twelve there was a short service with a sermon, at which the choir had no role. Vespers began at 1:15 with a motet. After various prayers and congregational hymns came a sermon, usually based on the epistle reading; the German Magnificat followed this. At the end, *"Nun danket alle Gott"* ("Now Thank We All Our God") was sung.

There was no specific Leipzig hymnbook; the congregation was presumed to know the hymns allotted to each Sunday.[10]

Whether writing church music for the organ or—as his duties took shape at St. Thomas—composing for orchestra and chorus, Bach almost invariably accepted, not chose, themes and texts. He was subject to the church calendar. The Lutherans observed holidays, of course, and even retained some of the Catholic emphasis on saints' days and events pertaining to Mary. Never "veneration"—that sticking point of the Reformation was anathema—yet the Lutheran church of Bach's day accorded more attention to, say, the Assumption than any contemporary Protestant denominations do. The *Magnificat*, which had been the traditional church's liturgical commemoration of Mary's visitation by the Holy Spirit and her humble response, was gladly taken up by Bach. The *Magnificat in D, BWV 243*, is one of the greatest works of his lifetime, a stunning document of faith and music for all time.

The church had prescribed many meditations and texts for the entire calendar year: holidays and feast days, of course; cycles revolving around Advent, the Passion, Easter and the Resurrection, Pentecost, and so forth. Continuing the use of signification and symbolism from the Middle Ages, the church used color in vestments and altar cloths to convey meaning and thematic preoccupations—white for the purity of the resurrected Lord, for instance; purple as reminders of the passion and royalty of King Jesus with the believer's response of contrition. Likewise, themes were assigned to every Sunday, indeed every service. Bible verses, entire passages, psalms, parables and epistles were all well chosen to structure the services, hymns, anthems and chorales, readings

(Old Testament, New Testament gospel and epistle readings), sermons . . . and music.

Bach seldom chose his own subjects, therefore, for cantatas. Whether he chose his own texts—librettos—is not always clear. The ecclesiastical theme for the day could be expressed by Bible passages, ancient letters or hymn verses to be reworked, even familiar exhortations. Sometimes Bach chose these; sometimes they were placed before him. Sometimes he wrote the libretto; sometimes he assigned it or "borrowed" from another church work on the topic. In the midst of this he never expressed any frustration or betrayed any creative claustrophobia. After all, everything was from the Lord's texts, biblically derived, and inspired by the Holy Spirit.

Bach's own notes, scribbled on the cover of a cantata score, provide his shorthand checklist of a typical Sunday's program:

Order of divine service in Leipzig on the morning of the first Sunday in Advent—The Prelude. Motet, Prelude to the Kyrie, which is accompanied throughout. Intoning at the altar. Reading of the Epistle. The Litany sung. Prelude to the chorale. Reading of the Gospel. Prelude to the principal music [i.e., the cantata]. The Creed to be sung. The sermon. After the sermon, as usual, some verses of a hymn to be sung, *Verba institutionis*. Then preludes and singing of chorales alternately until the end of the communion *et sic porro*.

For the churches, Bach's Leipzig period produced some of the most awe-inspiring music ever lifted to God. We have called

Leipzig Bach's "music box," his showcase. During his years at St. Thomas Church, Bach is estimated to have managed more than fifteen hundred performances (writing the music and performing at the vast majority) to an average audience of two thousand.[11]

Most of his 250 cantatas were composed and performed in Leipzig. Whereas he once composed a cantata a month to the astonishment of fellow musicians, at Leipzig he composed one a week over several periods. The mighty Passions, of which the St. Matthew and St. John survive today, were written for the St. Thomas Church. The majestic *B minor Mass* was written during Bach's Leipzig period. And, not forsaking "instrumental" music, he also wrote the *Goldberg Variations*, the second book of the *Well-Tempered Clavier*, *The Musical Offering*, and the *Art of the Fugue* during these years. Once again—as always—the quality was as impressive as the quantity. Many composers throughout history would be well satisfied to have composed just one of these creations in a career. Bach routinely wrote and wrote and wrote masterpieces.

All in all, from the smallest clerical duties to the highest profile position on church holy days, Bach willingly tended to the smallest details. In a radio roundtable Bach scholars recently discussed the two overarching functions he seamlessly fused:

> *John Kleinig:* So the Gospel, if you like, is proclaimed
>   by Bach as a cantor as much as by the preacher
>   from the pulpit.
> *Michael Marissen:* [Bach] is a very good preacher—what

a good preacher should be nowadays: comforting the afflicted and afflicting the comfortable. Bach is very good at doing both of those things.

Robin Leaver: So this is Gospel music, folks![12]

And so it was.

As Bach's service in Leipzig progressed, his duties remained varied and demanding, but he gradually devolved some personal management. At one point Bach sought, and received, a "side" appointment as honorary composer to the court of the Elector of Saxony in Dresden (whose realms included parts of Poland), which allowed him extra opportunities for composing. Indeed the *B minor Mass* arose from this appointment. Yet it seems Bach never intended to leave St. Thomas or Leipzig; the honorary appointment was a safety valve against any slights or pressures of his routine work in Leipzig. Throughout his career, to the extent he was a flinty employee, it is clear that Bach was motivated by a justifiable sense of pride—he was fully aware of his gifts—and a simple determination to be uncompromising about standards of quality when serving God.

Therefore, in a common phrase, he did not suffer fools gladly. Many of Bach's letters and his employers' surviving meeting notes, although they seem petty today, relate to disputes about incompetent staff or Bach's independence of action. Chief among the Bach biographers, Albert Schweitzer has argued that overall the composer's relationship with St. Thomas for almost three decades was amicable. Bach's outreach to the elector's court in Dresden was motivated by a desire for greater fame that would translate to more income and a broader platform . . . and respect. He waited for three years for an appointment from Dresden. In 1736 it came, and in the process he actually brought greater honor to St. Thomas and Leipzig, that their own composer was so honored by a major sovereign. Royal Court *Compositeur* was his title—honor of honors, for it indicated he had absolute free reign in what he wrote, as well as freedom when to visit and perform. He was like a composer laureate, an occasional guest conductor, in Dresden.

≈

Among the high points of Bach's activities during his time at St. Thomas Church in Leipzig, the first item on the list, if we could ask him, would be his family. He was exceedingly proud of all his children, not only the ones with musical talent—although most of them inherited the Bachs' musical talent as surely as other families passed buckteeth and freckles from one generation to the next. Barbara had given birth to seven children and Anna Magdalena bore him thirteen—with talented musicians among them as well.

The Bach household in Leipzig exuded *Gemütlichkeit* and activity: children coming and going, students practicing and boarding, visitors of all stripes, voluble dinner conversations, family reunions, and, of course, daily Bible studies, prayers, and evening hymn sings. In addition—would anyone think otherwise?—there was music, music, and music. In the Bachs' humble but spacious apartments he always had several keyboard instruments, including a harpsichord, a clavichord, and a now obsolete type of spinet that played very quietly—a keyboard instrument of Bach's design that sounded like a strummed lute (as personal and expressive as a keyboard instrument could be until the pianoforte evolved).

He practiced every day, and so did most of his children. He composed at night. Anna Magdalena and various children copied and transcribed his work. His daughters practiced their vocal lessons. Bach was particularly fond of the lute, the violin, his small keyboard, and the viola in his home setting.

We have mentioned the weekly salons at Zimmermann's Coffee House. Bach organized compositions and performances like the Coffee Cantata, other "secular" cantatas, small-scale church cantatas, and recitals of songs and instrumental music at a rate that would have exhausted many composers. And all this was extracurricular for him! Moreover, and this is a fact central to the understanding of Bach, whether these musical events, as head of the Collegium Musicum or independently, in meeting rooms, public gardens, or—often the case—in his own house, we don't see a man *needing* to get away from his job or his family. This was not escapism. Obviously the music was an extension of his regular assignments. It simply was what Bach *did*. In every activity his family participated, assisted, performed, or (to Papa's satisfaction) starred.[13] He loved and encouraged all his children equally, even a wayward son who left home and incurred debts (Johann Gottfried Bernhard) and a "problem child" (Gottfried Heinrich) who might have had the greatest musical ability of all siblings, but suffered some sort of mental disability.

Of the prominent musical children are two we have mentioned from his first marriage. Wilhelm Friedemann and Carl Philipp Emmanuel were excellent students who benefited from hearing more of Papa's music and receiving more instruction than did their siblings. Friedemann's talents seemed especially favored by his father and he became a prominent composer and performer. C.P.E. Bach likewise made a career for himself, although once admitting that he, like Friedemann, consciously strove to be different from their father.

Johann Christoph Friedrich Bach was concertmaster of Bückeburg's court, and Friedemann considered him to be the best keyboard performer of a sibling, particularly of their father's works.

Johann Christian Bach, first called "Bach of Milan" and afterward the "London Bach," was fifteen when his father died. He was least influenced and furthest musically, therefore, from his father. He became extremely popular in his day and exerted a major influence on the boy Mozart, whom he bounced on his knee. Some of Mozart's very earliest compositions—written when he was still young enough to be bounced on knees—were transcriptions of J. C. Bach pieces. A golden thread!

Two daughters—Catharina Dorothea, Bach's firstborn, and Elisabeth Juliana Friederica ("Liesgen") of the second marriage—were also accomplished singers and musicians who often assisted their father's work.

Bach and his wives managed what was by all accounts a busy, friendly, and spiritual household. Students sometimes lived with the Bachs. Family reunions—remember how large the musical Bach family was—were frequent. Despite the stereotype in some histories that the genius Bach labored in obscurity, his fame was widespread. If composers and musicians were traveling within a few days of Bach's residence, they always seemed to make a detour and meet the master, who was very welcoming and indulgent. Guests were invited to church and often they were induced to play the organ. Whatever the venue, visiting musicians often were invited to a contest or what today would be called a "jam."

In addition, with every job there were duties beyond writing and playing music. Often they included onerous chores. Many required Bach to address purely clerical or administrative, not musical, matters.

To understand Bach and his life we shall pause at these workaday concerns. "Christian encounters" do not always happen at great moments in history. God meets His children, and the faithful respond with integrity, in the routine times too.

≈

The German words for a "hometown birthplace" (*Heimat*), "homemade" (*hausgemacht*), "local" (*heimisch*), and "to bring home" (*heimbringen*), all employing the word *home*, indicate that the home is the center of social life in diverse ways. The church, as for centuries, was the focus of every town's activities, and a growing number of coffee shops and public gardens points to increased socialization. But home and hearth, kitchen and family room, is where families and friends gathered in friendship and fellowship.

This lifestyle provides a key to understanding Bach's music, its appeal, and even its purpose. The legacy of his church music, to use one measure, fills about half of his extant music, a yardstick of about 160 CDs (to employ a contemporary measure). Among his popular instrumental music are concertos, suites, and ensembles that, logically, are performed on concert stages. There are numerous instrumental solos and duets, and although some of these were meant to be instructional, they bring us closer to a vital characteristic of many Bach compositions that is easily lost in the context of recorded music, of stereotypical musicians in powdered wigs at royal salons. Many of Bach's works were written for friends and family, intended for home gatherings and for precocious young musicians.

To affirm the kinder and gentler personality of the Bach who otherwise stares at us—rather sternly—through history in two surviving painted portraits, we can look to accounts of family reunions of the Bach brothers, cousins, uncles, nephews, and children. These were at least annual affairs and were jolly, sometimes raucous, and always (no surprise) musical.[14]

Every festivity invariably began with praise music: a hymn or chorale sung by all members of the clan to a special arrangement or possibly a new composition prepared for the day. God was thanked for the blessings of the past year, and His blessings were invoked for the year to come.

Yes, there was food; yes, there was beer; yes, there was fellowship, gossip, and renewed acquaintances. But the highlight of every get-together was a good-natured "family feud"—a competition between each branch of the clan, employing what they called *quodlibets*, a Latin word. Today's equivalent might be "whatever!" or "as you wish." Each group prepared and rehearsed its own music for what became a "can you top this set?" sing-off. The only predictable or consistent aspect was the variety, but usually the music and words—and sometimes staged performances—were humorous. The Bachs were capable of silliness, sarcasm, nonsense—and sometimes bawdiness. In a family with so many music makers, history has recorded no instance of bitter rivalries between them or fallouts or jealousy![15] Surely their decent and civilized stock was not the sole reason for that, nor was music the only bond. A shared devotion to the Lord and a common and profound faith can explain much.

Similar to the *quodlibets*, the "Coffee Cantata" provides a glimpse of the informal and humorous Bach with his hair down (or wig off). The fact that it was likely first performed at Zimmermann's Coffee Shop, and that the beverage was sweeping Europe—an early-day version of Starbucks mania—obscures the fact that Bach composed it as an inside joke for his family. It was a humorous commentary on courtship more than coffee, and while never naughty—Bach never went there—it surely made some singers and auditors blush with its good-natured in-jokes about dating, marriage, and the dynamics of the Bach household.

So Bach could be funny *through* music, but he was always serious *about* music. His children were trained to sing and to play instruments, not just eventually to help their father in ensembles and transcriptions, but because they were Bachs! He trained and encouraged his daughters' talents and arranged that they appear in public.

There is visceral evidence of Bach the sentimental family man, of music meant for other than church or concert hall. It was early in his career when, in 1704, Bach's older brother Johann Jakob decided to serve as oboist in King Karl XII of Sweden's military band. Several Bachs, evidently including Johann Sebastian Bach, dissented from this choice, but when Jakob was set to travel north and take the assignment, his younger brother wrote the heartfelt *Capriccio on the Departure of My Beloved Brother*. An amazing testament to familial attachments, this was the closest Bach really came to "program" music (in the vein of Vivaldi's *Four Seasons* or Beethoven's *Wellington's Victory*), a beautiful and tender collection of pieces. It opens with a representation of Jakob's friends and family pleading that he remain among them. The following *andante* and *adagio* are emotional warnings of possible dangers and melancholia. A fugue then represents the several arguments of the coachman who agrees with the family's viewpoint, and so forth (to no avail)—a picture of family ties and heartfelt concern.

So, all the Bach household members went about making music. It was a "cottage industry" of sorts, but hardly cold or mechanical. Its creativity was earnest, pure, and, more often than not, spiritual. As we have noted, the second Frau Bach, Anna Magdalena, a superb copyist and a skilled musician and singer, is one of the reasons we have inherited so much of Bach's music. In 1722 Bach wrote one of his French suites for harpsichord, perhaps the most difficult of the series, in her notebook. Three years later he dedicated the group of intricate and masterful keyboard instructional pieces to her. The *Clavierbüchlein* [Little Notebook] *für Anna Magdalena Bach* still challenges, pleases, and amazes people today, almost three hundred years later.

~

The spiritual instruction of the Bach children was as strong at home as in schools, usually overseen by Frau Bach. The quality of the schools and choosing between his employers' schools or others in town always played a role in Bach's decisions to seek or accept postings. His children's education—spiritual first, then educational (for instance, Latin), then musical—was important to the father of this very large household. Of course, the "homeschooled" music instruction they absorbed and were assigned was, we reasonably can assume, world-class!

Bach read daily from the Bible and from Luther's works. If Bach was not strictly a theologian, we see evidence that he was indeed an ardent Bible scholar. He noticed that a certain respected scholar had

> missed part of Luther's commentary on original sin in Genesis 3. Luther had argued that original righteousness was an integral part of man, and Bach replaced the missing words from the Altenburg edition, where Luther illustrated the scholastic position of this righteousness as an adornment a man might place on a woman, "which comes from outside and without injuring her nature." Many other corrections

may be found in [the margins of Bach's copy], showing attention to detail, and a desire to understand his theology exactly as Scripture would have it understood.[16]

Bach was proud of his theological library, just as his musical library was known throughout Europe. Once he won a major collection of texts at an auction and jubilantly reported the purchase to a friend. He neither boasted nor complained about the auction price, but its receipt has survived; Bach paid the equivalent of a tenth of his annual salary for the books. Christoph Wolff noted that for Bach, "theological and musical scholarship were two sides of the same coin: the search for divine revelation, or the quest for God."[17]

Therefore, Bach stayed close to Christian music. The "secular cantatas" referred to above were the closest Johann Sebastian Bach ever ventured to the opera, the entertainment sweeping German lands and all of Europe at the time, and whose major composers were mostly Italian. The spectacle; the variety of comedy, tragedy, romance, or drama; the gaudy costumes and sets; the virtuoso performances, all attracted huge audiences and seduced many a willing musician. Some composers turned their attention to operatic forms, including large-scale overtures and musical declamations via recitatives and arias; some actually moved themselves to the center of action—Italy. Bach's *Landsmann* Georg Friedrich Händel was chief among the expatriates. In Italy he became Giorgio Federico Hendel, and when he moved to England to spend the bulk of his creative life, he was known as George Frideric Handel.

Whether Johann Sebastian Bach was too modest to follow the acclaim of the early-day "show business" lifestyle, or too fond of his native soil, or unwilling to long abandon the music of the church and such service to God—most likely a combination of all these factors—we are left with no operas by his hand. The "secular cantatas" performed at private venues such as Zimmermann's Coffee House, city gardens, and family events, however, allowed him to dabble in the form. It must be remembered that church work was, then as now for the most part, less remunerative than "show business." Bach surely was not unmindful.

One of the duties of a music maker who was also a family man was—and is—earning money. Bach had a larger household than most, and a busy guesthouse to maintain. There is a record of Bach's income at St. Thomas, likely his best-paid position. In a letter to his boyhood friend Georg Erdmann, Bach reported that his annual salary was approximately 700 Thalers (approximately $50,000 a year in today's money; note, by the way, that "Thaler" is pronounced "dollar," whence its derivation), yet, technically, only about a hundred Thalers was fixed.[18] It is certain that the council guaranteed a portion of the extra income, but it was likely unpredictable. Bach received a portion of the church's endowments and legacies, and he was allowed to charge fees for some instruction.

Most of the cantor's extra income derived from weddings and funerals, so there were reasonable, if not great, expectations; even in Leipzig people married and died. His fees, whether he composed or managed the musical aspects of these events, were based on the level of musical content—meager or elaborate. Bach frequently groused about couples who married in towns outside the city walls, where their fees were lower, and "economical" families who planned no-frills funerals for departed loved ones. The highest payment for weddings, he told Erdmann, was two Thalers; for funerals one Thaler, 15 Groschen (approximately $200 and $150, respectively).

Bach closed his letter to Erdmann with a remark either sarcastic or humorous, perhaps unconscious. It anticipates a scene in the W. C. Fields movie *The Bank Dick,* where Fields, as Egbert Sousè, asks the town doctor, "How's business?" The doctor replies, "Not bad," but adds with clear regret, "I don't suppose we'll ever have one of those whooping-cough epidemics again." In his 1729 letter Bach complained about the "clear [healthy] air," that fewer people were dying, and therefore his income was off a hundred Thalers!

The tendency of some biographers, particularly Albert Schweitzer, to maintain that Bach had a predilection to choose death and dying as his texts is not really supported by evidence. As we have noted, Bach seldom chose his texts, so his spiritual, or psychological, inclinations are not relevant to them. Perhaps his handling of death motifs resonates more than do others with some worshipers. If so, then his art receives the credit, not any morbidity to receive blame.

Further, there is no indication whatsoever in his private life or records or family recollections that Bach entertained any unique attitudes toward death and dying—that is, different from other Saxons or members of his family circle. Fully one-third to one-half of the local population had been lost in the late Thirty Years' War, it is true; and Sebastian and his two wives had lost more than half their children, eleven of twenty, to childhood death. In any event, these facts of life—war, disease, infant mortality—were not exceptional to those lives and in those times.

What seems clearest is that Bach, as a faithful servant of Christ and a learned inheritor of Bible promises and Lutheran doctrine, saw death as a glorious portal to paradise. He looked forward to the "many mansions" in God's house, the streets of gold, the believer's crowns, and the glassy sea before God's throne. As such a believer Bach naturally addressed the subject of death, when assigned to him, with general optimism and specific gusto.

There is no "if" regarding a special anointing to Bach's treatment of death. *Wachet Auf!* (Sleepers Awake!), about the resurrection of the dead; *Schlage doch, gewünschte Stunde* (Ring My Hour, So Long Desired); and *Komm, süßer Tod* (Come, Gentle Death), three of his many pieces on this theme, are supremely beautiful, precisely as the Bible intends such contemplation to be. It is possible that the analysis of Schweitzer—who confessed to seeing a mystical strain in Bach's faith—said less about Bach and more about Schweitzer.

Bach's humor, at family reunions, in secular cantatas, and—unconscious or not—in letters like the one complaining about the health and parsimony of townsfolk, affirms a joyfulness that is also evident in his music. The evocation of ecstatic dancing was discussed in the radio roundtable of Bach specialists we cited earlier:[19]

John Kleinig: Immense ecstasy, this is the thing that I find so fascinating about Bach. This sense of joy and ecstatic joy—of jubilation, in which we are in ourselves, and yet we are taken outside of ourselves into something that is far bigger and far better and far more wonderful than anything that we've yet experienced, intellectually, or emotionally or physically. It tries to give a sense of heaven here on earth: a foretaste of heaven on earth, but not in a life-denying kind of way. It bespeaks of the redemption of creation, not the denial of creation—that the physical world as we now know it is destined for something far bigger than we can imagine.

Robin Leaver: Bach "dances" in some of the most odd places. After Peter's denial in the *St. John Passion*, you have this incredibly intense aria, *Ach, mein Sinn*, where the tenor, representing Peter, is pouring his heart out. Yet, underneath it is an up-beat dance form. Though the voice is actually saying one thing—despair—the actual dance form is implying, "Ja, but it all comes out right in the end!" It is a basic dance form. You have the same at the end of the *St. Matthew Passion*; you have the final chorus, which, in a sense is a quasi-Sarabande [dance]. The text is about the sleeping Jesus—you know, the Jesus who has died and been placed in the tomb. The actual dance form is implying, "Yes, but there's more to come. What we can't deal with, because this is Good Friday, you'll hear about that in two days' time on Easter Day." Bach was not afraid to use dance forms and we know the people in Leipzig took dancing very seriously. And there were dancing masters around and they were very popular. People wanted to learn dance forms.

And when they were in church, here they were hearing Bach use dance forms in a remarkable way! I think what lies behind that is that it's a theological statement. I think it's a theology of the Incarnation, that Christ became fully human and that, therefore, all of human activities are transformed. Nothing can be considered outside the sphere of grace.[20]

When Bach's spiritual essence was acknowledged in secular assessments, it was validation, not contradiction. "Bach could spin music as a spider spins its nets, from earth to the sky and back again," wrote the greatest of American music critics, James Huneker.[21] "Bach, it is Bach who does it, Bach who animates the wooden, lifeless limbs of [composers of following generations], these modern men. Bach—once, last, and all the time."[22] He later paraphrased himself (when referring to Bach's *Well-Tempered Clavier*): "[It] is the Book of Eternal Wisdom. In it may be found the past, present, future of music. It is the Fountain of Eternal Youth."[23]

5

THE FIFTH EVANGELIST

The aim and final reason of all music should be none
else but the glory of God and refreshing the soul.
Where this is not observed there will be no music,
but only a devilish hubbub.

—Johann Sebastian Bach

B ach worked at St. Thomas Church in Leipzig nearly
half his life—almost 60 percent of his career—40
percent of his time on earth, twenty-seven of his
sixty-five years. It would be impossible for someone's work not
to undergo an evolution during such a period, and Bach's did.
He always tended to sum up rather than look ahead, and what
he rethought, reaffirmed, and rebuilt was not his body of work
alone, but vast traditions of ecclesiastical music.

Whether at church in front of a two-thousand-member congregation or in a prince's concert hall or at home with children, cousins, and friends, Bach—history's supreme music maker—went about his work the same way, believing himself called of God, honoring God in all things.

"Called of God." In Bach's case to believe so was not presumption. Seamlessly, he indeed considered his talent a calling. It was his duty—no, his privilege—to serve God by composing music, performing music, teaching music, conducting choirs, and arranging worship services. After all, they were reflections of God's creativity. Bach's own creative excursions went beyond tunes and melodies. He was driven to explore the technical limits of musical theory, to experiment and hone forms like counterpoint and the fugue, to discover the bases of musical science. And for no less a good reason than to serve the Lord better.

≈

In his last years he grew increasingly reclusive but certainly was not a hermit, because he had his daily duties as a worship leader. He did diminish his travel to learn from masters, however. *He* was now one whom musical pilgrims sought. Bach was never antisocial—indeed all evidence is to the contrary—and he clearly enjoyed the company of other musicians. It is supposed that during his last years he wrestled with theoretical music problems few others at that time could understand.[1] If anything, it was the rest of European music that had some things yet to learn from Johann Sebastian Bach.

But European music was less interested to learn from this master of the Baroque.

He made music and composed music. He continued to carry Christian worship to stunning and profound heights. All at a time when new musical styles—we can even say "fads"— swept the continent. Even his sons—garnering reputations of their own, continuing a Bach family tradition—were seduced by the light, airy, melodic styles of the day. The youngest, Johann Christian, who would eventually be called the "London Bach" because he conquered the British ears with Rococo compositions, was to refer to his father as "the old fossil." So if Bach was becoming estranged, it was the world that moved, not he.

This is not to suggest he was an outright anachronism, or a rejected museum piece. St. Thomas would not have retained such a back number and Bach was rehired year after year. His music continued to mature—more powerful, more abstract perhaps, but still impressing congregations and audiences. But there *were* new sounds in the land, catching the ears of the public.

Did Bach know that times were changing? Was he making a conscious decision to conclude his career by summing up both a mighty phase of Western music and his trademark synthesis of music and faith? It was nothing as egocentric as "building a legacy." That was never his manner. He might have been aware that things could die with him, however. Not just complicated musical styles or elaborate church services, but a unity of faith and creativity, an organic cohesion in cultural life.

Coincidentally, some later historians arbitrarily assigned 1750, the year Bach left us, as the closing date of the Baroque period; the end of an era; a pivotal moment in history. Modernism accelerated, the Age of Reason yearned for the Romanticism of a coming day, the Industrial Revolution was changing the dynamics of society, and faith itself was being challenged.

The last Leipzig years provide a clue to the essence of Bach's genius and his Christian service. He incorporated there the comprehensive details of his nationalistic impulses as well as the theological and worship traditions of his church. True to form, it was not a scrapbook of impulses he compiled; it was an immortality of sacred music that he achieved.

Bach taught mankind many things, but we must not lose sight of him as a teacher of ordinary students in the spare and drafty classrooms in Leipzig. Despite Bach's eventual delegation of many duties, teaching, and not just musical training, was central to his activities at St. Thomas School. Paul Nettl observed that this holistic educational philosophy of music is a thing of the past. Music was not a handmaiden nor a "vehicle" in Bach's time but a fuller, working partner, in the church service.[2] Grand music and humble lessons were coequal aspects of service.

In his three-volume biography of Bach, Albert Schweitzer devoted much attention to Bach's educational and classroom activities. "It is well known that Bach transcribed a copious amount of compositions by other composers. He enjoyed, of course, the arranging, adapting and correcting of these works, but he also felt a tremendous educational value in such an activity."[3]

Is it out of place to compare Händel and Bach (who are frequently compared) as football coaches—one who rushes to the professional leagues; the other who remains local, in the academic leagues, in part to educate, nurture, and influence young students? Händel looked outward, to the opera theaters of Italy and the courts of England. Bach looked inward, to tradition and to the German soil.

To assess Bach as a teacher we can turn to biographer Nikolaus Forkel, who interviewed many of Bach's students, thus providing us with as close an eyewitness account as we might have of Bach's personal techniques:

> Bach's method of teaching composition was . . . sure and effective. He did not begin with the dry details of counterpoint, as was the custom of other teachers in his day. Still less did he burden his pupils with the physical properties of sound, which he held to be matter for the theorist and instrument-maker rather than the composer. He started them off at once on four-part harmony over a figured Bass, making his pupils write each part on a separate stave in order to impress on them the need for accurate harmonic progression. Then he passed to Hymn tunes, setting the Bass himself and making his pupils write the Tenor and Alto parts. In time he let them write the Bass also. He insisted on correct harmony and on each part having a real melodic line. Every musician knows what models Bach has left us in this form. The inner parts of his four-part Hymn-tunes are so smooth and melodious that often they might be taken for the melody . . .
>
> Notwithstanding his strictness on this point, Bach allowed his pupils considerable license in other respects. In

their use of certain intervals, as in their treatment of harmony and melody, he let them experiment within the limits of their ability, taking care to discountenance ugliness and to insist on their giving appropriate expression to the character of the composition. Beauty of expression, he postulated, was only attainable on a foundation of pure and accurate harmony. Having experimented in every form himself, he liked to see his pupils equally adventurous.[4]

In some regards, of course, Bach's methods were idiosyncratic—reflections of his own training or his gifts. He was said, for instance, to regard musical parts in a composition as so many persons engaged in conversation.[5] There is no right or wrong in such matters when the factor of genius is considered, but what to *avoid* is forever good advice to any music student of any age.

It is instructive to take note of an assessment of the creative process by a composer whom many think is mankind's only worthy companion to Bach, Wolfgang Amadeus Mozart, born six years after Bach's death. He wrote to a friend:

I can really say no more on this subject than the following; for I myself know no more about it, and cannot account for it. When I am, as it were, completely myself, entirely alone, and of good cheer say, travelling in a carriage, or walking after a good meal, or during the night when I cannot sleep; it is on such occasions that my ideas flow best and most abundantly. Whence and how they come, I know not;

nor can I force them. Those ideas that please me I retain in memory, and am accustomed, as I have been told, to hum them to myself. If I continue in this way, it soon occurs to me how I may turn this or that morsel to account, so as to make a good dish of it, that is to say, agreeably to the rules of counterpoint, to the peculiarities of the various instruments, etc. All this fires my soul, and, provided I am not disturbed, my subject enlarges itself, becomes methodized and defined, and the whole, though it be long, stands almost complete and finished in my mind, so that I can survey it, like a fine picture or a beautiful statue, at a glance. Nor do I hear in my imagination the parts successively, but I hear them, as it were, all together. What a delight this is I cannot tell! . . . When I proceed to write down my ideas, I take out of the bag of my memory, if I may use that phrase, what has previously been collected into it in the way I have mentioned. For this reason the committing to paper is done quickly enough, for everything is, as I said before, already finished; and it rarely differs on paper from what it was in my imagination.[6]

The audacity of Bach's use of God-given talent can be gauged another way—briefly to mention some of his major works. In the following works Bach, characteristically, made significant contributions to Western music, solved problems that had plagued composers for generations, and left posterity with masterpieces that will live, in the words of H. L. Mencken, "as long as men have ears."

A SELECTION OF BACH'S MAJOR WORKS

THE WELL-TEMPERED CLAVIER BOOKS 1 AND 2

"Well-tempered" in the title refers to proper tuning. Many "temperaments" before Bach prevented compositions from moving through more than just a few keys. Bach's work (besides creating a fusillade of amazing music) changed the art of composition. The "books" are comprised of a prelude and fugue in each of the twenty-four major and minor keys.

THE GOLDBERG VARIATIONS

An aria with thirty variations named after a court musician who was charged with playing music so his sovereign could sleep. Bach composed a complex set of variations and canons, mathematically fascinating and beautiful, causing listeners today to wonder how anyone could sleep while hearing them.

THE BRANDENBURG CONCERTOS

To many people of our day, these are Bach's best-known orchestral works. They are not conventional *concerti grossi* (fast-slow-fast movements) but of various forms, featuring different solo instruments or just the *tutti* (chamber orchestra). They are so named because Bach submitted them in the hope of gaining employment from Margrave Christian Ludwig of Brandenburg-Schwedt in 1721. The job application, by the way, was unsuccessful.

THE FOUR ORCHESTRAL SUITES

Similar to Händel's *Water Music* and *Royal Fireworks* suites, these are stylized dances for orchestra, each opening with a French-style overture in fanfare. The familiar movement we know as the "Air on the G String" is the second movement of the *Orchestral Suite No. 3*.

THE PASSIONS

For Holy Week vespers services, Bach wrote the *St. Matthew Passion* and the *St. John Passion*, which were each performed for decades in Leipzig's St. Thomas and St. Nicholas churches on alternate years. (He periodically made improvements, especially to the *Matthew*, of which he was proud.) Three other *Passions* apparently have been lost.

ORATORIOS

Bach wrote several oratorios, the most magnificent of which is the *Weihnachtsoratorium*, the *Christmas Oratorio*. Its opening movement, *Jauchzet, Frohlocket!*, with timpani drums tuned to different notes, is among the grandest music Bach wrote. And the close of part two, *Wir Singen Dir In Deinem Heer*, seamlessly combining two previous beautiful melodies, is magical.

THE MAGNIFICAT

A short, majestic presentation of the angel Gabriel's visitation to Mary and her prayerful response to God's favor. This work stands alone in Bach's catalog, and nearly stands alone as a work among anyone's church music of any era. There were two versions, the D major version most heard today, and an earlier version in E-flat major, with four added Christmas-related movements.

≈

That Bach was a musical miracle of sorts is clear. Among his singular talents was an ability to compose as few others have done. Mozart—to whom we again turn for any reasonable comparison—similar to Bach, was able to listen to music and compose other music at the same time or grandly improvise from a simple tune, subtly incorporating it into an unrelated work. Both composers instantly solved musical problems over which other composers might have struggled for days.

There are many such tales with Bach. He had many keyboards in his office at St. Thomas and his apartment, but when he composed, it was often without benefit of any instrument. No experimenting, no testing. Even the most complicated multipart works flowed directly from his mind to paper. Many surviving manuscript scores reveal that first drafts seldom had corrections. There is an account that once he admitted (with due admiration) that he found a musical score he could not play at first sight. So, there we have it. Perhaps Bach was mortal after all.

THE TRINITY OF *C*s

As we have mentioned some of Bach's most significant compositions, we briefly will discuss what are possibly the three most significant modes (of many) he used to deliver his music and messages. (The reader is directed to Appendix C for fuller descriptions of Bach's formats and musical terms used in this book.) But the three musical tools most closely associated with Bach were honed during his time at St. Thomas Church in Leipzig, and understanding them helps us understand his music. They are the "trinity" of *C*s: counterpoint, cantata, and chorale.

COUNTERPOINT

Here is the ultimate deconstruction of Bach the composer—the "power of polyphony, an intrinsic harmonic structure, and an imaginative and original approach in the design of complex works,"[7] or counterpoint. This art of musical architectonics reached its apogee in Bach's works and has been used decreasingly by succeeding generations of composers. It is arguable that, besides the natural evolution of musical tastes and a desire to shed some of the density that characterizes counterpoint and polyphony, composers might have been intimidated to go where Bach had been. (It is also arguable that Western music, except for bright exceptions like Mozart and Beethoven, has been declining since Bach.)

Plato held up Harmony as a reflection of a Perfect Good that exists in the abstract, and because men should seek the Good, hearing it naturally pleases the ear, thence the soul. Music had evolved from strophes and unison singing through the Gothic era, when simple harmonies became standard. Polyphony, literally "multiple sounds," refers to the ability of several melodic lines, whether in straight harmony (relative to each other) or independent, combining to please the ear.

One step, actually many steps, further is counterpoint in the hands of Bach and his contemporaries. Music is built, Bach insisted to his students, on a foundation, a "ground," the bass line . . . the "figured bass."

Over this melody it should be possible to build another melody, even several, based on the harmonies of notes as you build upward on the musical staves. In so doing, the composer can construct several tunes that each can stand alone or harmonize, even despite great complexity. The forms of music today in which counterpoint heartily thrives are, perhaps, farthest found from concert halls. In ragtime and boogie-woogie the bass is a foundation that has a life of its own. In Dixieland and bluegrass the "parts" that different instruments play are melodies unto themselves. Having the closest affinity to counterpoint is Southern Gospel music, where four-part harmonies, always built on a strong bass line upward, follow (perhaps unconsciously) the rules of Bach. The primitive "convention style" singing schools and shape-note hymnbooks of the American South are vestigial descendants of Baroque counterpoint.

A canon is the strictest form of counterpoint, with a phrase repeated by other parts, in the same key, delayed and in sequence. "Row, Row, Row Your Boat" is the most common example. In a fugue, the most complex form of counterpoint, one part states a theme and, after the interval of a fifth, the second part takes up the phrase as the first part reverts to a "counter-subject." And so on to, usually, four parts. And in

Bach's hands the fugues could be a splendid complexity of mirror themes, "answers," reverse successions of notes, and so forth. And so forth!

Lending texture and richness is the application of broken chords, dissonances that resolve at proper moments, slightly delayed (or "robbed," *rubato*) notes, and so on. The harpsichord and organ, unable to effectively achieve loud and soft dynamics, present relatively equal prominence to all the lines from bass to soprano. But the bass line was always the foundation stone. There developed a notation system in German music, where numbers or symbols were written next to the bass notes on a score. They indicated to performers what harmonies or even countermelodies could be realized. Not an easy assignment. Bach did it unconsciously, without the aid of those symbols. The gift enabled him to read a melody line and construct a multipart composition on sight. It was a facility that amazed his peers.

Bach took this all a step further. He saw this musical architecture as more than something pleasing to the ear in the mysterious realm of music—the "universal language." Just as Plato saw symbolism in many things, Bach believed his "figured bass" theories to be a picture of God's creation: the Word was the foundation, and everything in life built upward—and should harmonize—with it.

Did some people then—do some people now?—criticize Baroque music for being ordered, logical, requiring our close attention? "Aha!" Bach seems to say through the years. "*Now* you begin to understand!"

In 1754, four years after Bach's death, his son Carl Philipp Emanuel collaborated on an essay, an extended obituary, in the journal *Musikalische Bibliothek*. About Bach's gift for counterpoint, the essay said:

If ever a composer showed polyphony in its greatest strength, it was certainly our late lamented Bach. If ever a musician employed the most hidden secrets of harmony with the most skilled artistry, it was certainly our Bach. No one ever showed so many ingenious and unusual ideas as he, in elaborate pieces such as ordinarily seem dry exercises in craftsmanship. He needed only to have heard any theme to be aware—it seemed in the same instant—of almost every intricacy that artistry could produce in the treatment of it. His melodies were strange, but always varied, rich in invention, and resembling those of no other composer. His serious temperament drew him by preference to music that was serious, elaborate, and profound; but he could also, when the occasion demanded, adjust himself, especially in playing, to a lighter and more humorous way of thought. His constant practice in the working out of polyphonic pieces had given his eye such facility that even in the largest scores he could take in all the simultaneously sounding parts at a glance. His hearing was so fine that he was able to detect the slightest error even in the largest ensembles . . . In conducting, he was very accurate, and of the tempo, which he generally took very lively, he was uncommonly sure.[8]

Alfred Einstein, author of *Genius in Music* and cousin of the famous physicist, wrote, "In everything he touched he said the last word. In the proper sense no fugues were written after Bach; actually, indeed very many more fugues were written, but none that went beyond the established requirements of the form. They merely filled out the form."[9]

CANTATA

We have mentioned the role of the cantata in Bach's weekly assignments and how it is almost synonymous with Sebastian Bach. As one of the three Cs of Bach's musical preoccupations, we will add a few comments.

Under Bach, the cantata became the central music of the church service. Hymns and chorales (especially) were not diminished in function, but the cantata took on an extra role, comparable to the sermon. Broadly speaking, the cantata was exegetical, *providing* the message, and the sermon was hermeneutical, *explaining* the message. Of course the Scripture readings and the liturgy, including creeds and confessions, were not diminished, but the cantata and sermon were the church's evangelistic engines of each service.

The cantata allowed Bach to use, with more room than in chorales and with more freedom than in Passions or oratorios, his musical symbolism—octave leaps, for instance, generally presaged a vision of heaven and earth. Again, it surprises many twenty-first-century minds to know that eighteenth-century believers understood these many motifs. No instruction manuals or subtitles necessary.

Most cantatas were written for specific days in the church year—and every Sunday *was* a specific day, with assigned texts and meditations. In Italian musical parlance, it was *Cantica di Tempore*—"cantata of the day." The preselected subjects of devotion were usually appropriate to the ecclesiastical season, sometimes dictated by long tradition. Any danger of rote, of growing stale from year to year, was mitigated by the spiritual passions of the congregation and the musical ministrations of such as Bach. Over his career he wrote five cycles of cantatas— a cycle comprised of a different cantata for every Sunday of the year! Unfortunately, only the equivalent of three cycles are extant. Counting cantatas written for special events, and a few "secular" cantatas, that translates to about 215 surviving from an estimated 300.

Having been entrusted with all these various but obviously important musical tasks, Bach magnificently achieved—week after week, year after year—what Schweitzer appropriately termed "sermons in music." Surely without any conscious-ness of such a goal, Bach's church music fulfilled the remaining agendas of the Reformation.[10]

CHORALE

In the chorale we meet a musical form, rich and expressive, with origins in the Gregorian chant, originally a plainsong or *cantus firmus*. In the Roman church it was associated with Bible texts or liturgical parts; Protestants tended to assign hymn verses and evangelical phrases. Eventually those distinctions dissolved, and multiple voices (hence "choral") and polyphony became hallmarks of the form. Almost inevitably, Bach was the church composer who brought yet another mode to its definitive state.

The chorale, unfortunately, has become a virtual museum piece, little heard today except in performances of ancient music, generally because its dedicated functions in church services, specifically the Lutheran service, evolved in a different direction. The longer cantata form was understandably retired, as the structure of church services inevitably changed. But the form and function of the chorale is still valid, just neglected.

One of the twentieth century's philosophical discoveries was Semiotic Theory—the science of signs and symbols—that addresses why we tend to respond to, and create, visual shorthand in many areas of life, primarily the graphic arts (think of symbols in comic strips) but especially in the plastic arts (for instance, the "language" of the cinema). We can think of the chorale, as Bach employed it, as aural signification and symbology.

That is, worshipers were familiar with a large group of hymns and gospel songs, and chorales drew upon the most familiar of these. A few notes, a couple of lines, a brief chorus in a new chorale, and worshipers immediately were reminded of the underlying meanings, recalling familiar songs and hymns. The chorale conditioned them to meditate on the Thought of the Day. Through a sophisticated nonverbal language of the chorale tune, they were cradled in the entire service's integrated message.

In Bach's hands these tunes did not signal "here we go again" or trot out an old theme song. Some of his most profound and beautiful music was in simple chorales. As always, he built from the bass line upward, and his harmonies were supernal. One or more themes—contrapuntally juxtaposed—formed a new creation. Familiar strains, whose meanings were hidden in the hearts of worshipers as surely as Bible verses were, formed the core of each chorale. Sometimes the musical phrase opened the chorale and transported the congregation immediately; sometimes it emerged from the sweet swirl of themes and embraced the worshiper. Many of Bach's chorales, unlike his other compositions, end in an ascending third note, a "deceptive cadence" that somehow surprises the ear with an uplifting feel of sunshine—the opposite of, say, minor keys or descending to minor notes, which strikes the ear as brooding or melancholic.

Beautiful in themselves, Bach's chorales are tender invitations to each part of the service they precede. It is hard to imagine any music more attractive and emotional. Bach soared to the realms of pure spiritual emotion. Most of the chorale preludes for organ and chorales for choir are between two and five minutes. He wrote hundreds of them, sometimes several based on one hymn or song.

To the less musically sophisticated—then, as now, probably the vast majority of worshipers—the chorales were simply beautiful music, basic but beautifully embellished tunes, perhaps known since childhood. We can think of "Praise God from Whom All Blessings Flow," "Now Thank We All Our God," "O God, Our Help in Ages Past," "Holy, Holy, Holy," or "Fairest Lord Jesus" and imagine tuning in to the message's total import. Would Bach be amused that some twenty-first-century churches think they have discovered the way to bombard the senses with multimedia presentations? The practice, if not the effect, of repeated themes has evolved somewhat through the centuries. Dr. Bill Bright once told me of his displeasure with "7-11 music" in churches, by which I thought he meant the bland, Muzak-style of song. He explained that no, he meant the bland music that consisted of "seven lines, repeated eleven times."

Many of the hymn texts and poems Bach chose to use were written by Martin Luther, "A Mighty Fortress Is Our God" chief among them. Bach also favored the works of two Christian mystics. Philipp Nikolai's, for example, *"Wie schön leuchtet der Morgenstern"* and *"Wachet auf, ruft uns die Stimme"* ("How Brightly Shines the Morning Star" and "Wake, Awake, for Night Is Flying") and Johann Franck's *"Jesu, meine Freude"* ("Jesus, Priceless Treasure"). He also used Bible passages and homilies dating back before Luther. The tunes largely were time-honored favorites of the church but included ancient chants and folk tunes as well, all having some spiritual touchstone.

Bach built chorale preludes, for instance, around two different musical treatments of "By the Waters of Babylon," by Johann Pachelbel and the Hamburg's venerable organist Johann Adam Reincken. It is interesting to hear that biblical theme today—and in some permutations, the old musical themes themselves. Singers as disparate as Paul Robeson, Bob Marley, and Willie Nelson have sung "By the Waters of Babylon," although the German title—*"An Wasserflüssen Babylon"*—somehow has a different resonance when sung by such performers. Yet there is a thread.

Bach mastered another technique that anticipated psychology—the subliminal message, a goal of later tone poets. Like no one before or since, he used musical keys, notes, themes, motifs, cadences, rhythms, instruments, voices, and ornamentation as tools to create moods, suggest messages, and plant ideas in the listeners' minds. For example, any composer would naturally choose a harp to suggest something angelic, or trumpets for martial airs. Bach, however, adopted or rejected elements in order to create a total effect: *Gestalt* before its time. He used instrumental "phrases," not only instrumentation, to suggest the dramatic content of a spiritual text.

Two examples will illustrate his use of music as melody and music as symbolism. In the cantata *"Gottes Zeit ist die allerbeste Zeit"* ("God's Timing Is the Best Timing"), the text quotes from Revelation 22:

> [These words] were in the composer's imagination, and inspired that unique tone-picture where the lower [musical] parts, still muttering the stern decree of fate, at last mount gently in triads (while the strings have a passage in contrary motion) and vanish like clouds into the air, while the soprano—supported by a bass, the pulsating rhythm of which grows ever fainter and fainter—hangs alone over the abyss like a fluttering spirit, and when at last all has become still as death fades away, gently murmuring the name "Jesus."[11]

Similarly, in the *Magnificat*, when Mary confesses to being blessed among all generations, Bach creates a cascade of voices (*Omnes generationes* in Latin) ascending, descending, echoed, choir parts in multiple layers, until we have an almost visual picture of heavenly hosts.

In instrumental pieces, Bach did not just write notes, but always was respectful of the distinctive sounds and effects of instruments. If the viola da gamba produced a timbre he deemed appropriate for a certain sonata, for instance, he would not write it for its cousin, the violoncello. This is why his keyboard works never sound right on the piano, Glenn Gould's famous interpretations notwithstanding.

≈

Counterpoint, cantatas, and chorales—they are by no means *all* of Bach; but if one had to write on the palm of the hand his three favored modes as a composer, the three *C*s would fit perfectly. Yet Bach cannot be pigeonholed. His excursions to many expressive forms are breathtaking. James Huneker observed that mankind does not *know* things, as a rule; it rather tends to *name* them. Bach's catalog is almost bereft of love songs, despite a few *Lieder* that prefigured those of Mozart and Schubert. But of course the correct view is that everything Bach composed was a love song—to God.

6

THE MESSAGE IN MUSIC

[The organ] is to be played with both hands in such a manner that the left hand plays the prescribed notes; the right hand, however, executes the consonances and dissonances so that a pleasing harmony will result to the honor of God and the soothing delight of the spirit.

—Johann Sebastian Bach

Ludwig van Beethoven once said, making a pun on the meaning of *Bach*—a stream or brook—"Not a stream but an ocean!" History, as we shall see, caught up with the "historical postulate" that was Bach. But in his own day, toward the end of his Leipzig days, his reputation somewhat morphed from a vibrant genius to something of an abstract curiosity. The public taste was changing and what was desired in concert halls and opera theaters was felt in churches too. People seemed ready to turn the page on the Baroque style, even in the worship music and structure of church services that Bach had honed and owned. Changes are inevitable in music as with most things in life; for good or ill, tastes change.

But we are reminded of the soundness of Baroque music in general, and Bach in particular, when we consider that some of the changes in the musical world were "crutches" of the sort to which Bach seldom reverted. Some composers develop their own distinctive musical devices—stylistic conventions that sometimes die with them. Other conventions overtake a period of music, often become out of fashion, and ultimately are more crutches than solutions in the composer's craft.[1]

For instance, an otherwise obscure Italian composer, Domenico Alberti, is credited with standardizing an innovation in playing bass chords on the keyboard in Classical (post-Baroque) music. Instead of playing three notes as a chord, the "Alberti Bass" makes a quick arpeggio of low-high-middle-high notes. It makes for a livelier and richer sound. Some composers disparaged it as a wearying trick device, but all composers have used it in some fashion, from Mozart to boogie-woogie. Rococo and Classical composers also fell back on the "Mannheim Crescendo," a coda that concludes musical phrases and themes—or entire movements—universally used by Mozart and Haydn and early Beethoven, last heard, perhaps, in Rossini. It is hard to call such a pleasing musical turn a crutch, but it provided a template for composers that, overall, had not been available to Baroque writers. Bach, of course, employed the Basso Continuo[2] or Figured Bass, but as many composers and performers will attest, this was hardly a crutch.

There have been other musical clichés through the years. Many popular songs end with the rhythmic "shave and a haircut, two bits," the familiar knock on the door. Cha-cha-cha endings solved many dilemmas for composers of popular and dance tunes. The "back beat," a delayed accent of percussive timing that rock composers Lieber and Stoller claim to have introduced—and lives today, almost obsessively, in Contemporary Christian Music— was clearly a template. John Lennon once provided a recipe for rock 'n' roll: "Just say what it is, use simple English, make it rhyme, and put a back beat on it," which recalls Harlan Howard's definition of country music, "three chords and the truth." There are *expectations* our ears have in recent musical styles—rhymed lyrics, rhythmic structure, chord and melodic progression[3]—that simply were not employed in Baroque music. It might not mean that Bach's successors were musically lazy, but it certainly means that Bach continually was more inventive. He had to be.

~

The timeline of Bach's jobs reveals that, despite the small circle of his travels and a decision to forsake venues like opera and theaters, he managed to touch many bases. He composed in many styles, mastered many categories, and faithfully served God at every stop. The making of all music—for worship or purely instrumental pieces, in choir lofts, public gardens, or home settings—was unto the Lord.

By some reports, Bach filled twenty pages of music a day, seldom using a keyboard or stringed instrument for testing or experimenting—going straight to paper—and seldom making corrections or cross-outs on the score. There could not be a better temptation to call Bach's talent inspired. Many of Bach's works live today in the basic concert repertoire, hymnbooks, CD sales, and mp3 downloads. He probably wrote eighteen hundred to two thousand separate works, approximately twelve hundred of which have survived.

He was a busy family man. He instructed a great number of students, including his talented children, in composition and performance. As a freelance, a provision permitted in every job he held, he hired himself out as composer and musician for weddings, funerals, and town festivals. He was a consultant to organ makers and organ repairmen. He tested, endorsed, and sold keyboard instruments, from quiet spinets to multimanual harpsichords. He offered vital suggestions for the design and manufacture of the earliest pianos, although he was not enamored of their sound, and he invented a keyboard instrument that sounded to listeners like a lute. "His artistic creativity," in the view of biographer Christoph Wolff, sometimes "border[ed] on the incredible."[4]

Bach's diminishing duties toward the end of his career at St. Thomas were due less to employers' displeasure with his work and more to a natural management style. A generation of assistants had grown up under Bach. "Retreat but not rest" is how biographer Christoph Wolff characterized Bach's last decade.[5] In his last decade of life he composed fewer short works, reworked many of his own pieces from previous years, and worked on some monumental pieces that hint to us of an emerging desire to compose summaries of all that his career represented. Bach also dealt with the factor of encroaching blindness, a physical handicap for composers whose threat was second only to the deafness that plagued Beethoven and Fauré. But gloom did not overtake his cheerful personality nor his aggressive creativity. While he served his God and was surrounded by his loving family, how could it be otherwise?

≈

We have noted Bach's almost superhuman creativity. As his career at Leipzig was winding down—as his musical production was changing its character in his last decade—we can survey Bach's larger contributions. His output was almost exclusively Christian or instrumental music—no opera, no ballet music, no dance music for the stage. He occasionally incorporated folk music but shunned popular tunesmithing, and he never based music on drinking songs or "bar music," as urban legends claim about Luther and him. In today's parlance, he "restricted his playlist." Church music and instrumental music inhabited his only "houses"—but in his houses there were many mansions!

His church music spanned the wide range of styles and modes, from traditional chorales to introspective motets, hymns and congregational songs, fanfares and sinfonias for church services, liturgical music and calls to worship, cantatas whose movements were interspersed with parts of the Lutheran service, full-fledged Masses, oratorios (on the scale of Händel's

Messiah, so familiar to audiences today), dramatic Passions, and immortal versions of standard church music like his *Magnificat*.

Bach was more than a mere devout composer of clever music. He was an evangelist who used music. For all of the liturgical forms in which he worked, he mastered other significant forms of composition as a pioneer, or, more likely as the last word in those genres. Biographer and musical historian Christoph Wolff has limned some of the conquered categories, and Bach's chief works therein. Earlier we mentioned some of these compositions in the context of their fame or impact. Here (a different way to see—or hear!—them) they are categorized by the modes they exemplified: [6]

- fugue and canon: *The Art of Fugue*
- major-minor tonality: *The Well-Tempered Clavier*
- harmonic expansion: the *Chromatic Fantasy and Fugue*
- extended polyphony: the suites for unaccompanied violin, cello, and flute
- instrumentation: the *Brandenburg Concertos*
- instrumental and vocal genres: Bach employed virtually all contemporary models and types—from aria, *cantata burlesque*, and canzona to oratorio, scherzo, and sinfonia
- small-scale form: the *Orgelbüchlein* (Little Organ Book and suites for lute)
- large-scale form: the *St. Matthew Passion*
- stylistic and compositional range, from retrospective to modern: the *B-minor Mass*
- musical effect and exegetical meaning: the church cantatas

As noted before in a different context, any composer in history would have been satisfied to master just *one* of those genres.

THE KING OF INSTRUMENTS

We have reserved a discussion until now of an aspect of Bach's art that, despite his many other monumental achievements, looms above all else, a monolith that sometimes seems to dwarf other instruments, other ensembles, other means of expression: the organ.

We have noted that the organ was Bach's first instrument. His famous works and greatest technical achievments were as an organist early in his career, and it was on basis of that reputation that at St. Thomas in Leipzig he oversaw organists and was not obliged to perform, although he did at every opportunity. Therefore his compositional focus was elsewhere. Bach revered the "king of instruments" through the Leipzig period, however, until his last day. We recall that magnificent organs and legendary organists betook him on foot journeys as a student, far away (relatively speaking) from his home. His first jobs were primarily as an organ player. For a teenager to receive such appointment affirms his aptitude. His first dispute with employers occurred when he took four months instead of four weeks to visit a famous organ and famous organist. Some of his earliest compositions were for the organ. As we sum up the Leipzig years and Bach's career, the organ, appropriately, must provide the accompaniment.

Bach and the "king of instruments" had a natural—we can almost say an unnatural—affinity. He became as one with the instrument. The more complicated its console, the more at home he was and the more astonishing was the music that flowed from the mighty pipes. How providential of God to plant Bach in the region where the grandest pipe organs in history flourished.

Another feature naturally attracted Bach. The organ, more than any other instrument before or since, is the essential music maker in church worship. Many American churches are trying to become comfortable with drums and electric guitars, but their permanence is not assured. The organ reigned for centuries. Bach both inherited and bequeathed the relationship between Christian worship and the church organ. Strings and brass and reeds and drums and voices—more and more voices, including the Lutheran penchant for congregational singing—also were Bach's inheritance. As organs grew larger and more complex throughout Europe, "schools" (that is, distinctive performance styles) arose in England, Holland, Denmark, and north Germany particularly.

As the king of instruments evolved into massive blast furnaces of sound and fury, Bach, as much as any composer, also wrote concert pieces, affirming his unified view of spiritual and "secular" music. What home or town hall could accommodate one of these musical behemoths? So, for purely instrumental music, that is, organ music not related to a hymn or service—for instance, sonatas, fanfares, concertos, and fugues—churches allowed recitals for the public.

Organs grew so imposing and multifunctional that some players disdained many of their features and potentialities. Organ builders were known to be relieved when churches considered scaling back their plans, and repairmen occasionally allowed some options to go fallow. Bach's own son, Wilhelm Friedemann, an excellent organist, said that sometimes he went a whole year without using the foot pedals! Mighty bellows had to be pumped by hand to power the instrument's sound; therefore Bach's irreducible assistant was always a bellows-boy. Larger organs had as many as five manuals (keyboards), each with a different function. Most organs had foot pedals, but those in larger churches required something akin to choreography to master them. Usually the pipes were arrayed behind the organ—that is, facing the organist. In larger churches some pipes were bundled in various places around the sanctuary, nave, or transept. Surround sound!

Through the years many of Bach's "homes" as a conductor of worship, a cantor, were in organ lofts, on balconies behind the congregation. The balconies faced the altar and he played the organ and conducted with his back to the church or off to the side, from the keyboard or, technically, the manuals. Where there are foot pedals, manual playing is a separate activity for the hands, hence the name. On each side of the grander organs were dozens and dozens of "stops," or pull-buttons, each with distinct function but in two classes. Some stops work as dynamic devices, like pistons or couplers, to strengthen or diminish the organ's volume. Other stops—the pride of craftsmen—could make the organ mimic a variety of other instruments: trumpets, trombones, flutes, oboes, bassoons, old airy sackbuts, percussion, and all manner of sounds.

Because an organ is different from a piano—their similarities suggested by rows of black-and-white keys, but they go their separate ways after that—mechanical innovations were needed to achieve dynamics. Without such tools even the harpsichord could approach more aural diversity. With them, however, the organist is able to sustain notes, simulate echoes, and so forth. In addition, the organist's fingers must behave differently than the pianist's. Added pressure on the keys, for instance, by itself has no effect on the loudness of the resultant sound. The Baroque organ's hundreds of keys, stops, pedal boards, drawknobs, drawbars, registration controls, swell-pedals, couplers, pistons (tremolos), registration presets, and a variety of manuals with names like Solo, Great, Choir, Echo, and Swell seem as complicated as today's jet cockpit control panel.

The cavernous cathedrals and sanctuaries that arched upward and stretched forward, simulating the grandeur of God's heaven to individual worshipers, found their logical counterpart in magnificent, mighty organs. As the organ clearly represented to Bach the musician's ultimate instrument of praise, however, Bach the organ player represented something more ambiguous to those around him. For Bach suffered the lot of many geniuses through history: he often was misunderstood. His compositions left some listeners behind. Church officials, usually musical amateurs, marveled—but did not always approve.

Schweitzer provided accounts of his organ playing:

Whenever it suited him, he could realize such astonishing, exciting, and lively chords at the organ through the use of his feet alone (whether or not he was playing anything else with his hands) that another could never quite imitate him even by playing with the hands. Once, when he was invited from Leipzig to Kassel to dedicate a reconstructed organ, he ran over the pedal-keys with such agility that his feet seemed to be winged.[7]

The organist and musical historian Heinrich Fleischer—who was born in the Eisenach of Luther and Bach, and attended the same Latin school—noted in 1950 that listeners, according to his research, time and time again "were astonished by [Bach's] extraordinary choice of organ registration and his imaginative selection of tone color."[8]

Part of Bach's almost extrasensory genius was his ability to reckon the acoustics of a sanctuary or cathedral, or any room. Nikolaus Forkel, who wrote the first major biography of Bach, having spoken with many of the composer's family members and associates, reported:

When he was at Berlin in 1747 [Bach] was shown the new Opera House. He took in its good and bad qualities at a glance, whereas others had done so only after experience. He was shown the large adjoining Saloon [concert room] and went up into the gallery that runs round it. Merely glancing at the roof he remarked, "The architect has secured a novel effect which, probably, neither himself nor any one else suspected." The Saloon, in fact, is a parallelogram. If a person puts his face to the wall in one corner of it and whispers a few words, another person at the corner diagonally opposite can hear them distinctly, though to others between them the words are inaudible. The effect arises from the span of the arches in the roof, as Bach saw at a glance. These and similar observations suggested to him striking and unusual combinations of organ stops.[9]

Bach was able—according to this account, by remarkable instinct—to adapt his compositions and performances to accommodate the echoes, for instance, and how certain notes and tones "worked." He realized how long notes took to fade in the far corners and upper levels of a church or theater and played accordingly. Bach's son Carl Philipp Emanuel, who ought to have been jaded by years of witnessing his father's genius, nevertheless wrote in awe years after Bach's death: "He heard the slightest wrong note even in the largest combinations. . . . Thanks to his greatness in [counterpoint], he accompanied trios on more than one occasion on the spur of the moment and . . . converted them into complete quartets, astounding the composer of the trios."[10]

A contemporary account continues:

His method of registration [programming the stops] was so unconventional, that many organists and organ builders were horrified when they saw his selection. They believed that such a combination of voices [organ sounds] could not possibly sound well, but they marveled when they later noticed that it was exactly in this way that the organ sounded its best and that it had only received something heterogeneous and unconventional which their own manner of registration had lacked.[11]

Nikolaus Forkel offered other anecdotes—testimonies of listeners lost in admiration, and organ makers frozen with terror:

Strangers often asked Bach to play to them between the hours of divine service. On those occasions he was wont to select and treat a theme in various ways, making it the subject of each extemporization even if he continued playing for two hours. As a beginning he played a Prelude and Fugue on the Great Organ. Then he developed it with solo stops in a Trio or Quartet. A Hymn-tune followed, whose melody he interrupted in the subtlest fashion with fragments of the theme in three or four parts. Last came a Fugue, with full Organ, in which he treated the subject alone or in association with one or more accessory themes . . . [When testing an organ Bach frequently] drew out all the stops, to hear the Full Organ. He used to say jokingly, that he wanted to find out whether the instrument had good lungs! Then he gave every part of it a most searching test . . . Such demonstrations of his powers invariably invited the verdict, that he was conclusively "the prince of Clavier and Organ players."[12]

Despite his justifiable pride and realistic assessment of his prowess, his innate modesty once caused Bach to reply to a compliment: "There is nothing remarkable about it. All one has to do is hit the right notes at the right time, and the instrument plays itself."[13] This modesty, surely genuine and not a pose, is nearly a cipher to our contemporary culture. That Bach's life was humbly and totally given to God—not in spite of but because of the talent that could have led him anywhere in the musical world, to courts and theaters and opera houses—provides the twenty-first century with a model to admire and emulate.

A BRILLIANT SUNSET

With devotional music, God is always present in
His grace.

—Johann Sebastian Bach

Bach produced two works in his final years that are stunning in their scope and mastery of form, rather than betraying any evidence of an aging composer's diminished powers. It is noteworthy that neither work was produced on commission or assignment, not from St. Thomas Church nor the court in Dresden, and each was specifically created with the intention of honoring God in unique and rather unorthodox ways. In this particular we plainly see little difference from the spiritual mode of Bach's entire life and career. But during their creation, these works seemed to be as between Bach and God. Bach finally achieved introspection, but it was to be in music, not journal entries.

The two works are also significant in that they did not roll from brain to paper. In fact, they took years of contemplation, writing, and revising, through the Leipzig period. They are vital yet dense in the best sense of the word; they excite the emotions but are cerebral. Devoting years to their composition, Bach determined them to be statements, to be comprehensive in everything they addressed—which was much—and he meant to write them unto the Lord.

The first was the *Mass in B minor*. Bach wrote it in the fashion of the traditional Catholic Mass, restoring portions Lutherans usually omitted or reserved for other sections of the service, such as the *Credo* (Creed). Bach contemplated no mutiny from the Lutheran ranks. He was, rather, paying homage to centuries of Christian worship. In some parts of this Mass, he went back to medieval and Renaissance inspirations; in others, he borrowed from works of his own career, so it was written anew but was assembled from various sources and inspirations over twenty years. He prepared it most earnestly before his death, in 1748 and 1749, truly a *summum opus*—his highest achievement, literally a "summary" work.

B minor was Bach's favorite key in which to compose,[1] and this was only one of many symbolic statements and meaningful motifs in the work, all pointing to messages Bach needed to express, as if he were a fervid evangelist, before he died. Spitta wrote:

> The *B minor Mass* exhibits in the most absolute manner, and on the grandest scale, the deep and intimate feeling of [Bach]

as a Christian and a member of the Church. The student who desires to enter thoroughly into this chamber of his soul must use the *B minor Mass* as the key; without this we can only guess at the vital powers which Bach brought to bear on all his sacred compositions.

When we hear this Mass performed under the conditions indispensable to our full comprehension of it, we feel as though the genius of the last two thousand years were soaring above our heads. There is something almost unearthly in the solitary eminence which the *B minor Mass* occupies in history. Even when every available means have been brought to bear on the investigation of the bases of Bach's views of art, and of the processes of his culture and development; on the elements he assimilated from without; on the inspirations he derived from within and from his personal circumstances; when, finally, the universal nature of music comes to our aid in the matter, there still remains a last wonder—the lightning flash of the idea of a Mass of such vast proportions—the resuscitation of the spirit of the reformers.[2]

The B minor Mass was never performed in full during Bach's lifetime, and indeed never until the next century. That is, on earth.

Very similar dynamics—an apparent summing up, simultaneous abstraction and accessibility, the culmination of many years' work—apply to Bach's *Die Kunst der Fuge* (*The Art of the Fugue*).

Contrary to traditional assumptions, *The Art of the Fugue*

was not a deathbed composition. Bach had begun work on it in the early 1740s. Nevertheless he constantly revised it, almost to the time of death. He was preparing its publication when he died; he never quite finished the work; and he never indicated the scoring! We do not know whether Bach meant *The Art of the Fugue* for solo harpsichord or organ, or small ensemble or chamber orchestra.[3] But it was counterpoint—that most complicated, and most Bachian, of Bach's modes—taken to the heights. *The Art of the Fugue* is not just a pinnacle of Bach's career; it is a highpoint in the sweep of Western culture.

Neither the *B minor Mass* nor *The Art of the Fugue* was composed on commission, as we noted. "It is mainly due to the inner urge to produce," wrote Alfred Einstein. "Nothing *forced* Bach to write."[4] It was the same motive-force that drove Mozart to write his symphonies 40 and 41, at a time of financial distress, with absolutely no commissions or performances in sight, as well as his six quartets dedicated to Haydn. And why Händel abandoned the opera and turned to the oratorio later in life.[5] The Divine impulse.

⁓

The Rococo period, led particularly by the French and the Mannheim School in southwest Germany, eschewed the heavier, almost mathematical, aspects of Baroque music. It elevated melody over structure. It was "light." Bach and his style of music were honored in memory but, astonishingly, largely forgotten for a generation after his death in 1750. *O tempora! o mores!* (Oh the times! oh the manners!)

It was all the sweeter, therefore—and most appropriate—that Bach was able, in the closing years of his life, to receive an honor unique in his time and, literally, his place. Bach's son, Carl Philipp Emanuel, was prominently employed as a musician by Friedrich der Große—Frederick the Great of Prussia—whose glittering French-style court, Sanssouci in Potsdam, was becoming a cultural hub of Europe. Frederick was a respectable composer and an accomplished flautist and had long pressed his court composer C.P.E. Bach to bring his legendary father to the court's music chambers. The prospect of inspecting recently invented pianos helped lure Bach in his sixty-second year to the court outside Berlin.

We have noted that, although Bach moved up the ladder of prominent posts and assignments, and enjoyed a reputation as a master of all he surveyed, he never strayed more than approximately three hundred miles from his birthplace during the course of his sixty-five years. Technically speaking, Bach was a regional phenomenon. His fame was widespread, yet he never sought celebrity; and it scarcely was accorded him. In a bizarre race against time, the musical styles he inherited, transformed, and owned were becoming obsolete at the time of his death. Certainly the artistic foundations themselves could never become obsolete. At least *one* person recognized that in Bach's waning years, and he was an important admirer. Hence Frederick the Great cast himself almost in the role of a fan, as we would say today, as he anticipated Bach's visit.

Old Bach and his son Wilhelm Friedemann arrived at the king's residence, and before he had time to change from his traveling clothes, Bach was rushed into the music hall, a flattering welcome accorded by the monarch. Bach played the pianos to the astonishment of everyone. The prototypes were not unknown to him, as he had advised their inventor Gottfried Silbermann. Frederick presented Bach with a random but challenging musical phrase, several notes upon which Bach improvised a three-voice fugue. Frederick "upped" the creative ante and requested that Bach devise a six-voice fugue. Bach gladly accepted the challenge but asked to go home to realize it properly.

Two months later Frederick the Great was significantly impressed to receive an incredibly complex set of fugues (properly, canons), a four-movement trio sonata for flute in honor of the king, and "musical riddles" over whose scores Bach wrote how rising notes, ascending modulation, and so forth, all made specific allusions to the king's fortunes. Everything was based on the simple musical phrase the king provided. Bach not only wrote this astounding body of work, but also had it engraved and printed at his own expense. Today we know it as *The Musical Offering*.

Accounts of the visit and Bach's amazing achievement were published in journals all across Germany. The royal invitation and the recognition of Bach's creativity added to what was, in itself, a high point of Bach's musical life. That a war recently had been waged between Prussia and Saxony is sometimes forgotten by history. Frederick the Great was another rare benevolent monarch, but the fact that Bach accepted this invitation six months after the king's triumphant troops had withdrawn from Leipzig cast the musician in the additional role of peace ambassador.[6]

It is possible that some of the court's hangers-on tittered behind their gloves that this *burgher* type in his dusty traveling clothes, even playing amazing intricacies on the spot, was a throwback, maybe an *idiot savant*. But Frederick the Great knew who graced his presence. Bach's sons knew. And by newspaper accounts, all of Germany knew—it was sweet to smell the roses. Always secure in his talent and grateful to God for his gifts, old Bach knew too. His own "coda" was three years away, but all of his creative affairs were being put in order.

The world might well find Bach's music easy to understand but hard to explain, as we noted at the beginning of this book, but it could never be in doubt as to his Christian faith, nor his musical credo. As historian Heinrich Fleischer wrote:

> He gathered in the harvest not only of the experience of his own life, but also of the entire period of [Western] Christian music . . . He grouped together the choice hymns of Luther in the form of a Mass and composed them in the manner of the old masters. So he established an immediate bond with the contrapuntal and spiritual ideal of the Middle Ages and the Reformation. During the last years of his life he revised earlier organ chorales and only then gave them their timeless and lucid form.[7]

In Bach's final days, he composed one last piece of unique music, a grand fugue based on the letters of his name—B A C H—"as unto the Lord." In German musical notation *B* indicates B-flat, and the letter *H* stands for B-natural. More than a clever conceit or attempting a musical pun, it is clear that Bach knew he was writing his last earthly music—not *about* God, but *to* God. This man who dedicated his life to God by dedicating his life to music, all in humble conviction that God had gifted him specially, composed a complicated fugue based on the very letters of his name. That is, lifting high his very *life*, a thanks-offering to God.

As the world's music had grown more sophisticated, complex, and beautiful, it was the counterpoint and fugue of the High Baroque that represent the purest science of musical composition. Now Bach turned it all back to God, interwoven as it always had been, with his life, his talent, his last breaths. And what of the art and craft of music? To many people, despite some melodies, power, and emotion of music that followed down to today, it cannot be called progress.

Those four notes—B A C H—played together, ascending, descending, forming themes and mirror themes, in harmony and contrast, swirled upward, upward, from the humble cantor's rooms in Leipzig, Germany, to the Creator God who allowed His humble servant Johann Sebastian Bach the privilege of transcribing His music for a brief season.

≈

This very last work was even more a significant offering to God—and a message to us. Because Bach was completely blind in his last four months, he had to dictate this last piece, a chorale, no easy task under any circumstances. Everything about it was appropriate in this most appropriate life of Christian encounters, even the dictation itself, because many people behold Bach's vast lifetime accomplishments as those of a man who took musical dictation from the Lord.

In the darkened room, to his son-in-law and pupil Johann Christoph Altnikol, Bach dictated a chorale, the form that Bach revered as the Holy Spirit's shorthand notes to mankind—a short work based on a familiar church melody. Like much of the *B minor Mass*, it was built upon a tune by Martin Luther, which brought things full circle. The spiritual guide whose folkish roots were the same as Bach's, and whose Christian revelations lit his pathways, inspired Bach's last music. The final chorale's text referred to Death, never an unwelcome theme for Bach, and now, he sensed, his next guide. It was based on the chorale prelude "*Vor Deinen Thron tret' ich hiermit*" ("Before Your Throne I Now Appear"). It recalled the musical tradition of the north German homeland whence he came, and again firmly embraced the legacy of the medieval and Reformation chorale motet, but elevated to timeless significance.[8]

> When in the hour of deepest need
> We know not where to look for aid;
> When days and night of anxious thought
> No counsel yet have brought,
> Our comfort then is this alone:
> That we may meet before your throne
> And cry to you, O faithful God,
> For rescue from our sorry lot.
> Before your throne I now appear,

Oh God, and humbly plead:
Turn not away Your gracious face
From a poor sinner such as I.

The verses have different attitudes toward the approach of death, as music historian Peter Billam observed:

The first [thought] sings of deepest distress, and the second of something far more glorious. So Luther's tune itself is ambiguous . . . The moment of death can be seen as painful, or as glorious; by his choice of notes Bach makes clear his point of view . . .

The intensely clear personal expression arising from the assumption of difficult technical constraints, the modesty, and yet also the [audacity] of composing with only Martin Luther's notes, the wonderful beauty of the piece and the personal circumstances under which it was written, combine to make this chorale prelude one of the greatest achievements of the Western musical tradition.[9]

We cannot help but notice that chorales of this sort—of any sort—are no longer composed and seldom performed. There is no reason it must be so; but the modern and postmodern cultures have frozen as if in amber such precious creative expressions, forms that can be counted among our civilization's great accomplishments. Alfred Einstein sadly noted, "Anyone who composes [in the style of Bach] today commits an anachronism"[10]—which is less an observation about contemporary composers than a sad assessment of contemporary culture's standards.

≈

In Leipzig, old Bach's eyesight steadily deteriorated in his last years. From reading descriptions of his symptoms, some believe that cataracts were the culprit. At the time it was thought that his boyhood proclivity of copying scores by the moonlight had weakened his eyes. Ironically, Bach's *Landsmann* Händel, in London, was also losing his sight.

These two great composers, born within months and miles of each other, never did meet. Bach issued one invitation and at another time had to miss an appointment because of ill health. Legends have arisen about Händel being dismissive of Bach's obscurity or of his fear that Bach might challenge him to a keyboard competition, but they are groundless legends. However, the two composers were united in having to confront blindness in their final years—and being mistreated by the same doctor.[11] Händel was visited a year after Bach's death in Leipzig by the itinerant English eye surgeon whose questionable efforts relieved neither composer's affliction and who might have hastened Bach's demise.

In early 1750 a one-man medicine show, "Chevalier" John Taylor, appeared in Leipzig. A surgeon of dubious skill, he ultimately confessed to blinding hundreds of patients. At that point, near death, he ironically was sightless himself. He was, at least, an accomplished self-promoter. He rode across the continent in a wagon painted with eyes and the legend "Giving Eyes Is

Giving Life." His method was to charge patients what the traffic would bear, including jewelry, and he usually ordered bandages to remain over patients' eyes for many days, by which time he frequently had ridden out of sight—all too often, literally. Yet he talked a good game, cited endorsements of celebrities from England to Persia, and occasionally attained happy results. He remains an ambiguous figure in his field, for amid his chicanery he developed some legitimate procedures, for instance, the surgical approach to strabismus by means of cutting an eye muscle.[12]

Taylor pulled into Leipzig at a time when Bach's family and friends were extremely concerned about his near total loss of sight. It is not recorded whether the composer freely or reluctantly agreed to go under the Chevalier's knife for what was diagnosed as a cataract problem. Operations took place in the last week of March and first week of April. A follow-up was deemed necessary because of an apparent reappearance of the cataract; Taylor somehow was still in the neighborhood. In a procedure known as "couching," Bach sat nearly upright in Taylor's specially constructed chair and was constrained by an assistant. There were no anesthetics and, of course, any movement by the patient was dangerous.

Cataracts and knives possibly were Bach's least worries. Taylor practiced bloodletting, the prescription of laxatives, and eyedrops custom-made from pigeons' blood, sugar, and salt. His bandages were infused with baked apples. Family members later spoke of Bach's severe pain after the operations and of "complete blindness" in both eyes. There were also accounts of Bach's four final months of life, wracked with ocular pain and fevers. A few days before his death on July 28, his family reported that his sight returned for a few hours, and then some sort of stroke eased his departure from this life.

Johann Sebastian Bach was mourned for his musical work and for his Christian faith. But Bach's work and Bach's faith were not just intertwined; they were *one*. That is the point of Henry Adams's profile of the average believer from the "Dark" Ages in *Mount St-Michel and Chartres*, his monumental book about medieval art and faith. Common believers, aided by informed spiritual guides from the creative world and presented with art and music and worship that is organic, of one accord, can attain a profound faith. Those ancient peoples "got it." And that is the testimony of Bach's work and his life. If this bedrock unity of life, faith, and art were similarly alive in today's culture, widespread and undisputed, we might not have felt the need to stress the positive phenomenon so often in these pages.

In the contemporary secular culture, Bach's sacred works are often treated like aesthetic curiosities, great works of art—but only that.[13] Bach, of course, would be offended by this. He was devoted to doing the Lord's work! It is ironic—but exceptionally revealing—that simple folk of Bach's day, and humble Christians through the following years, sense a connection with an artist devoting his gifts to his Creator; and that the "elite" of the contemporary, secular culture have a congenital inability to even conceive of such a person. For example, a review of Christoph Wolff's book *Johann Sebastian Bach: The Learned Musician* by Edward Said included this assessment:

Bach remains the pious-seeming Christian, which is how all of his interpretive biographers, especially Albert Schweitzer, have persuaded themselves to see him. Yet there is something unmistakably demonic and frightening about his fervour. Of course, he worked on his study of technique and on his scores, but in almost all of them he achieved feats of creativity that must have left him deeply impressed by his own gifts. One can't help wondering whether all the piety and expressions of humility before God weren't also Bach's way of keeping something considerably darker—more exuberant, more hubristic, verging on the blasphemous—at bay, something within himself, which his music with its contrapuntal wizardry also communicates.[14]

To the contemporary culture, Bach is not pious but "pious-seeming." Biographers didn't recognize but "persuaded themselves" that he was a faithful Christian, that his talents were not anointed of God but "unmistakably demonic," that "impressed by his own gifts" his ego engaged in an internal rivalry with God. Such a pathetic worldview is not a valedictory to Bach but an epitaph of the postmodern critique.

We do not need filters or interpreters, however. We have Bach himself to refute the ignorant and the willfully malicious. "One of the very interesting features of Bach is that one of his favorite books is Ecclesiastes," another contemporary—an admirer—has noted. "One of the things that's emphasized in the book of Ecclesiastes, and you can see the marks in the columns of his copy of the *Calov* Bible . . . is that God gives us work to do, for no other reason than to share His joy with us. That's a theme that runs all the way through Bach's work."[15]

8

BACH TO THE FUTURE

Besides other forms of worship, music has . . . been
ordered by God's Spirit.

—Johann Sebastian Bach

Many things died with Johann Sebastian Bach when
his soul went home to be with the Lord on July 28,
1750.

It is easy to start a list and difficult to stop, when con-
sidering how much has changed since then. The Declaration
of Independence in the far-off American colonies was still
twenty-six years in the future. The French Revolution, which
turned Europe on its head, was almost forty years away. The
Enlightenment and the Industrial Revolution were barely
under way, their ultimate effects impossible to imagine from

the vantage point of a small city in Saxony. Wars would again ravage the continent, but in ways unimaginable to Bach's generation. The arts would undergo radical change—here Bach *did* have an inkling—but the time was passing when artists and composers and poets, thinkers and philosophers, even theologians, assumed *a priori* that God was at the center of the universe and their own pursuits.

In many ways, not just concerning music theory, Bach was the last of the Old Man Men in Western culture. In foundational terms his music built upon the rules of the Middle Ages and Renaissance: his Baroque style was the quintessence—not the rejection, but the fulfillment—of Western music's foundations.

In his theology Bach was an Apostolic Age, no-frills, New Testament believer, with the reformist zeal and clarity of his guide, Martin Luther.

Bach would be shocked by postmodernism and, of course, neither was he a modernist. Like Isaac Newton and several other theocentric beacons of the Enlightenment era, Bach can perhaps be seen as one of the last premoderns. Luther, reformer and liberator in so many ways, was yet a fundamentalist of faith who said, "Reason is the greatest enemy that faith has: it never comes to the aid of spiritual things, but—more frequently than not—struggles against the Divine Word, treating with contempt all that emanates from God."[1]

The "S.D.G." (*Soli Deo Gloria*—to God alone the glory), with which Bach ended so many musical scores, takes on an extra meaning to us through these perspectives. Most people, especially devout Christians of the twenty-first century, understand *God* and understand *glory*. But it is hard for us today to understand how a man like Johann Sebastian Bach could say and mean *alone* in that Credo. Emerging cultures and emerging churches have compartmentalized every aspect of life, including God. Personal fulfillment is the artist's goal in today's world. To Bach's worldview, such a concept was an offense to God. God alone is the source, the content, and the goal of artistic expression.

"Great art in the service of high religion is foreign to us [today]," wrote O. P. Kretzmann, president of Valparaiso University, critically adopting the "voice" of contemporary culture.

> We cannot love the music of Bach because we do not share the faith of Bach. In the truest sense of the word his approach was sacramental. He used the mechanics of music—the arduous task of composition, the limited but honest resources of the eighteenth century organ, the oboe, and the harpsichord—as means to an end. Under his heart and hands, they became vehicles of a faith that used them to their highest potentiality. They now spoke of God, of life, of death, of faith, of hope, of atonement and forgiveness in terms so sure and magnificent that our anxious and questioning age hears only faint and far trumpets from a forgotten country.[2]

In the end, questions about Bach's music being easy or difficult to understand pale beside the challenge of whether citizens of the twenty-first century—even devoted Christians—can fully appreciate his type of faith. Christians who lived before Bach include first-century believers and martyrs and the faithful of the early church, pilgrims and missionaries of the "Dark Ages," those who broke their backs eking out existences in medieval villages so they could devote even more time and treasure to the church, artists and craftsmen, architects and builders, carvers of stone and wood, copyists of sacred manuscripts, crusaders and reformers dedicated to Christ. It is arguable that Christians who lived *before* Bach would understand his faith more easily, more quickly, and more comprehensively than Christians of our time, despite all of our time's knowledge and sophistication.

To the extent that is true, Bach's music meets us as more than stunning works of art. His works confront us, as does his life itself, as a challenge. John Kleinig, professor at Luther Seminary in Adelaide, Australia, said:

> Bach's music . . . challenges much of our whole modern worldview, our whole modern way of thinking and feeling and acting. It calls into question the things that we regard axiomatic. And to some extent, therefore, it is a "thorn in the flesh." It is a provocation. It shows us, at a time when we are reduced to individuality and many little sub-cultures, the possibility of being part of something much larger. And in that sense, Bach, like any great artist, reads *us* and interprets *us* and challenges *us* and provokes *us* and demands a response *from* us.[3]

Nietzsche assessed Bach in 1878, and complained: "In Bach there is too much crude Christianity, crude Germanism, crude Scholasticism . . . [A]t the threshold of modern European music . . . he is always looking back toward the Middle Ages."[4] How ironic that, as countless Christians of his own time and our time misunderstand Bach, a notorious atheist and cultural cynic describes him perfectly! Bach did not appeal to Nietzsche, obviously, but his assessment was on the mark. As for the "crudity" Nietzsche observed, he should have known that many foundation stones are rough-hewn.

Kleinig sees a somewhat different Bach:

[Bach] wants to draw us into some sense of enjoying God as God enjoys us . . . into [a holy] dance! . . . This is shown most clearly in the *Mass in B minor* in its ascending and descending movements. And probably most of all in the great Sanctus, where we are taking out of ourselves and into God; and the joy of God, and this enormous sense of exuberance and ecstasy that takes us out of ourselves and into something that is far bigger, more capacious and wonderful than the wonders of creation. And the beauty of it is that it never becomes disincarnate. It never becomes disembodied. You don't go up on a ladder into heavenly realms, but it's all here and now. It's firmly rooted in the body, in physical rhythms, in the rhythms of breathing, in actual physical sounds and physical things. Whether it's creation or whether it's the physical part of worship, bread and wine, water, words, musical instruments, all those kinds of things,

it's all very, immensely physical . . . It's immensely sensual.
And that's one of the things that's so pleasing about it. It's
intellectual, it's sensual, it's emotional somehow—all the
human faculties come together in embodied form."[5]

And on those wings the music, if not always the message,
of Bach survived the changing musical tastes of his last days and
his relative and temporary obscurity. It caused the generation
after him to discover and honor him, albeit in small numbers,
first among connoisseurs and the fraternity of composers.

～

For a generation following his death, Bach was virtually
unknown outside of his musical offspring and students. The
fashion of new musical forms, a new direction in his church's
liturgical fashions, and a near-universal societal desire for
change relegated him to obscurity. Remember, this was the
dawning of the age of the American and French revolutions.
Amazing. Gradually, however, through the nineteenth century
people discovered and embraced his music anew. His hymns
were made permanent parts of hymnbooks of various denominations, and composers of all styles and schools were awestruck
by Bach's mastery of the "science of music."

In 1781 the Gewandhaus of Leipzig that, still today, is a
shining light of musical excellence, had Bach's portrait painted
on the ceiling of its new concert hall. It happened that, whether
by the small number of printed works or a respectful word-of-
mouth, Bach's star was rising by the end of the century. Or—his

"sun" was rising. An illustration in the influential periodical *Allgemeine musicalische Zeitung (General Musical Newspaper)* in 1799 depicted a sun with many rays emanating from it. Some of the German musical names it displays, for that is the visual allegory, are forgotten today (Seidelmann, Stölzel, Graun); some are respectable (Gluck, Schutz, Telemann); others are, by anyone's consensus, great (Händel, Mozart, Haydn) . . . but at the center of the sun is the name "Joh. Sebastian Bach."[6]

Bach's greatest advocate during these years was, in fact, a forgotten hero to whom gratitude is due in musical culture. Baron Gottfried van Swieten (1734–1803) mightily changed the direction of music between the Baroque and the Romantic periods. Dutch-born as his name indicates, he was reared in Austria where his father was personal physician to Empress Maria Theresia. Gottfried became a diplomat, the Austrian ambassador to Prussia after the Austro-Prussian war, and then became a royal librarian in Vienna and a patron of the arts. Van Swieten discovered, celebrated, and publicized the music of previous generations, particularly that of Bach and Händel. He subsidized Mozart, Haydn, and Beethoven, whether it was (respectively) in times of need, managing oratorio productions, or launching a career.

Mozart discovered Bach through van Swieten's collection of scores and was thunderstruck by the theories of counterpoint. Van Swieten had Mozart arrange the version we know today of Händel's *Messiah*. Beethoven dedicated his *First Symphony* to van Swieten. The baron commissioned Bach's son, Carl Philipp Emanuel, to write his own greatest works, the *Six Symphonies*.

And van Swieten was behind the writing and publication of Nikolaus Forkel's landmark biography of Bach (1799), which is properly dedicated to van Swieten. Because of the baron's affection for Bach and weekly parlor concerts in his home, Haydn, Mozart, and Beethoven became virtual acolytes of Bach. Because Bach's approach to counterpoint profoundly changed their own work, all Western music that followed thereafter was affected.

Then, we might say, the floodgates were opened. The great German writer Johann Wolfgang von Goethe discovered Bach's music and described it: "Eternal harmony carries on a dialogue with itself on what God felt in his bosom shortly before the creation of the world." The composer Felix Mendelssohn Bartholdy, a Lutheran converted from Judaism, was awestruck by the *St. Matthew Passion* and staged a legendary performance on Good Friday 1829. Its revival was repeated and Mendelssohn brought his enthusiasm for Bach to England, where he was a favorite of the German-descended Queen Victoria (of Saxon and Hanoverian royalty). Bach's music was also a model for Mendelssohn's early church music, despite being written on the threshold of the Romantic era.

Music historian Clemens Romijn has traced just some of the major figures in music whom Bach influenced in the years intervening since his death. One does not have to be a musical sophisticate to grasp the sweep of Bach's influence over the entire, and almost unending, musical landscape:

Without Bach, Haydn's late string quartets and Mozart's latest symphonies and *Requiem* would have sounded quite different. Beethoven, Mendelssohn, Schumann, Chopin, Liszt, Brahms, Debussy, Reger and Hindemith too played and unraveled Bach's works, nourishing their own style and feeling very small next to Bach. Carl Maria von Weber considered Bach's music to be so new and perfect that everything before him lost its significance. Brahms claimed that, if he had had to compose Bach's *Chaconne* for solo violin, he would have become so shocked and wound-up that he would have gone mad. The pianist and conductor Hans von Bülow believed that if all classical music would be lost and only Bach's *Well-Tempered Clavier* would survive, all music could be built up again from it: "*The Well-Tempered Clavier* is the Old Testament and the Piano Sonatas of Beethoven the New; we must believe in both." And Debussy said: "Bach is Our Dear Lord of music. Every composer would do well to pray to him before commencing work." For many composers and musicians the motto has indeed been "not a day without Bach." The last project completed by Claude Debussy before he died of lung cancer in 1918 was an arrangement of Bach's Sonatas for viola da gamba and harpsichord. The world-famous cellist Pablo Casals [who once called Bach "my best friend; he is the god of music"] began each of his days with a piece from *The Well-Tempered Clavier* in order to imbibe, to absorb, something of Bach's genius.[7]

The great American music critic James Huneker was a devotee of Classical and Romantic pianism and wrote hagiographic biographies of Liszt and Chopin. Significantly, in his first book of essays (1899) and his posthumous collection (1921), bookends of fifteen other books and countless essays, he praised Bach as utterly unique in the pantheon of music: "Great, good, glorious, godlike Johann Sebastian Bach, in whose music floats the past, present, and future of the tone art. Mighty Bach, who could fashion a tiny prelude for a child's sweet fingers, a Leonardo da Vinci among composers, as Beethoven is their Michelangelo, Mozart their Raphael."[8] He advised every aspiring pianist: "Play the Chopin etudes, daily, also the preludes, for the rest trust to God and Bach. Bach is the bread of the pianist's life; always play him that your musical days may be long in the land."[9]

Many later composers not only incorporated his rules of counterpoint, but in singular homage, even built works around the notes B, A, C, H. His youngest son J. C. Bach led the list, followed by Schumann, Liszt, Rimsky-Korsakov, Reger, Busoni, Nielsen, Honegger, Schoenberg, and Webern.

The Bach *Gesellschaft* (Bach Society) was founded in 1850 to celebrate the master, and it has been chief among scholars who have continually analyzed Bach's work—even to studying the watermarked paper and ink components of his scores—and updated the catalog, which is known by *Bach-Werke-Verzeichnis*—the "BWV" numbers appended to all his music.

In the 1870s the monumental biography by Philipp Spitta was published, three volumes of analysis, musicology, and history. Bach had arrived, as Spitta set the standard for appreciation and further scholarship. Andre Pirro, *L'esthetique de Jean Sebastian Bach* (1907) and Albert Schweitzer, *Johann Sebastian Bach* (1905–1911, cited herein), extended the study of Bach to more poetic and practical considerations, with emphasis on vocal and organ works.

≈

Today there are hundreds of Bach societies and Bach festivals around the world. In 1898 the little town of Bethlehem—not of the Christmas carol but of the Pennsylvania steel mills—commenced its annual Bach Festival. Like the Oberammergau Passion Plays, indeed like most of the performers at Bach's several churches, amateurs are the featured players and singers. And, as in Bach's churches, the spirit of both Christian love and folkish amity reign.

Even the patented cynicism of the brilliant writer and critic H. L. Mencken could not hide adoration of Bach's music. Mencken returned year after year to the Bach Festival in Bethlehem. Excerpts from columns he wrote in the 1920s include:

> What, indeed, is most astonishing about the whole festival is not that it is given in a Pennsylvania steel town, with the snorting of switching-engines breaking in upon Bach's colossal Gloria, but that it is still, after all these years, so thoroughly peasant-like and Moravian, so full of homeliness and rusticity. In all my life I have never attended a public show of any sort, in any country, of a more complete and charming simplicity . . . The singers are businessmen and

their stenographers, schoolmasters and housewives, men who work in the steel mills and girls waiting to be married. If not a soul came in from outside to hear the music, they would keep on making it just the same, and if the Parker Memorial Church began to disturb them with echoes from empty benches they would go back to their bare Moravian church . . . It is indeed not a public performance at all, in the customary sense; it is simply the last of this year's rehearsals and as soon as it is over, next year's begin.[10]

In journals devoted to Bach, debates about restoring and properly playing vintage instruments were largely solved by the Polish keyboard artist Wanda Landowska. A century ago she discovered, restored, and rehabilitated the virtually extinct harpsichord through the music of Johann Sebastian Bach—actually in order to revive the music of Bach. Besides bringing untold masterpieces to light in the standard repertoire, she single-handedly—or, technically, two-handedly—deserves honor as the artist who first let us know how ancient music sounded. The great lady once said, "You play Bach your way and I'll play him *his* way." It is now uncommon, almost inviolate, not to record vintage music on period instruments and, unless such instruments or their reconstructions are unavailable, in performance as well.

In 1940 Walt Disney's *Fantasia*, an animated feature cartoon that aspired to, and achieved, avant-garde brilliance, opened with a visual tour-de-force of explosive and cascading colors to accompany the musical tour-de-force of Bach's *Toccata and Fugue in D minor.* The program book, by music critic Deems Taylor, said of their treatment, performed by Leopold Stowkowski and the Philadelphia Symphony Orchestra, that is, Stowkowski's august orchestration of the organ score:

> This magnificent work offered [the Disney animators] their greatest problem. Here was music that bore no title, beyond a descriptive one, music that evoked no definite action, told no story . . . This being abstract music, let it be projected on the screen in abstract images.
>
> Imagine, they said to themselves, that you are sitting in a concert hall, listening to this music with your eyes closed. What images does your mind conjure up? At first, presumably, you will be more or less conscious of the orchestra. And so, as the Toccata begins, the images on the screen are impressions of the orchestra itself, fantastic ranks of violins, cellos, and basses, flashing before your eyes as they take on the burden of the theme, shadows of the players in superimposed ranks, green, blue, red, purple shadows, row upon row of them. The fugue begins, and the images become less and less concrete. Are those violin bows flitting like sparrows across the screen? They move in circles, then divide and cross as the voices of the orchestra cross in unison with them. Now heavy cloud forms drift across the screen, and strange vaporous shapes that wind and undulate like sky-writing.
>
> Then a curious, rippling mass that might be a brook, or a sand dune in motion. The theme is announced. Something like a comet flashes across the ripples. The answer. Another

comet streaks past, in the opposite direction. Slowly the cloud masses gather into what might be a gigantic set of organ pipes. The fugue reaches its peroration. With the last, gigantic, organ-like chords the clouds dissolve into a blaze of light, against which stands the tense, vibrant silhouette of the conductor. A last great chord. Bach has spoken.[11]

By the 1960s, when *Fantasia* enjoyed a subsequent and profitable release to theaters filled with hippies mesmerized by the abstract amalgam of music and art, Johann Sebastian Bach seemed to be everywhere. Walter Carlos, programming and "performing" on the Moog synthesizer, scored a tremendous hit with the album *Switched-On Bach*. The Swingle Singers, from France, likewise sold many albums, starting with *Bach's Greatest Hits*, *Going Baroque*, and *Back to Bach*—music that the Swingle II ensemble still performs today in its inimitable scat-singing jazz. Another Frenchman, Jacques Loussier, merged Johann Sebastian Bach with cool jazz in a series of innovative albums, *Play Bach*.

Nonesuch Records released an album of impressive Bach translations played on electric guitar by Andre Benichou and His Well-Tempered Three, *Jazz Guitar Bach*. Turning the tables on the turntables, the Joshua Rifkin album *The Baroque Beatles Book*, songs of the Fab Four as Bach would have scored them, achieved great acclaim. Pablo Casals, who had performed Bach's *Unaccompanied Suites for Cello* at the White House under Theodore Roosevelt, reprised Bach's music at an evening musicale for the Kennedys.

The actor Brian Blessed portrayed old Bach in *The Joy of Bach*, a 1978 motion picture that was minimal biography and maximal celebration of his music, with clips of choirs from Bach's own St. Thomas Church in Leipzig; St. Olaf college in Northfield, Minnesota; St. Paul's Church in Manhattan; and the all-black Brooklyn Boy's Chorus. Also shown was the Moog synthesizer, alone in a lab but emitting glorious fugues; the pop concert organist E. Power Biggs, playing Bach under a light show and leading his audience in a college-style cheer, B! A! C! H!; disco dancers gyrating to adaptations of the master's work; the U.S. Marine Band and the Canadian Brass going for Baroque; a Caribbean steel band adhering, actually, to the proper notes and cadences of Bach's beautiful music; and pianist Rosalyn Tureck, founder of the International Bach Society, playing Bach on harpsichord, the more personal clavichord, a piano, and an electric keyboard. The film features the gifted guitarist Chistopher Parkening performing difficult transpositions of Bach's harpsichord work to the guitar.

In the contemporary sense, Johann Sebastian Bach fully arrived as a cultural icon when in 1977 the *Voyager* spacecraft was sent to nowhere in particular except up, with the hope that, hurtling beyond the solar system and maybe the galaxy, it might meet some alien civilization in a remote part of the universe. Perhaps, it was hoped, aliens would discover and understand something of mankind from the spacecraft's unique payload—a copper and gold alloy disk, estimated by its designers "to last a billion years," whose first selection was a recording of the *Second Brandenburg Concerto*, first movement, by Johann

Sebastian Bach, performed by Karl Richter and the Munich Bach Orchestra. How ironic if the faraway civilization were to have nothing but 8-track or cassette players on its planet! Among the playlist of global music, Bach was the only composer represented thrice. The gavotte from the *Violin Partita No. 3* and a prelude and fugue from *The Well-Tempered Clavier*, Book 2, were the other pieces chosen to represent humankind's creative profile. Biologist Lewis Thomas was asked what he would have nominated for this message to unknown civilizations. "The complete works of J. S. Bach," he said. "But that would be boasting."

In the book *Bach and the Heavenly Choir*, published in Germany after World War II, author Johannes Ruber speculated that if Bach had been a Catholic instead of a Lutheran, he long ago would have been canonized.[12] Indeed the fuller acceptance of Bach's sacred works could draw the two communions closer in these times.

In its 1968 Christmas-season issue, *TIME* magazine, no stranger to its own brand of canonization through its "People of the Year" issues, placed a portrait of Johann Sebastian Bach on its cover and ran a major essay on him, "The Fifth Evangelist." The 1980 Pulitzer Prize for Literature was awarded to Douglas Hofstadter's *Gödel, Escher, Bach: An Eternal Golden Braid*, "a metaphysical fugue on minds and machines" built on the works of the transformational legacies and putative common themes of, respectively, the logician, the artist, and the composer.

Bach's music has prevailed in the musical world, even in countless unknown ways. But his message—his Lord's message—sometimes seems lost in the din, a different cacophony than he could have imagined. Kretzmann wrote:

> The world of 1750 was a comparatively quiet world in which the music of a man, singing greatly to his God and Savior, could be heard and loved by men and women who lived and believed simply . . . When they heard *Gottes Zeit ist die beste Zeit* they understood the music and the message . . . But even more tragic is the amazement of the [contemporary] mind when it is confronted by Bach, the man of faith. What shall the new pagan do with a man who so magnificently fused high art and high religion? Or how can many modern Christians, accustomed to shoddiness, emotionalism and subjectivity in their religious life, understand a man who humbly accepts the great objective truths of Christianity and pours them into music which makes them live and breathe and march into the souls of men? That sort of thing is beyond us.[13]

Not every believer has had a road-to-Damascus moment like St. Paul's; nor a terror-filled lightning storm in the Thuringian forest, where Luther vowed to study for the priesthood; nor a direct battle with Satan, as Luther did, in the famous legend where he threw an inkwell at the enemy while translating the Bible in the Wartburg Castle in Eisenach.

Sebastian Bach was born into the Lutheran faith, died a committed Lutheran communicant, and, by all evidence, never experienced any spiritual doubts or crises of faith. His employers were largely ecclesiastical, and his few secular (court music) postings always included Christian music in their assignments. Fully half of the music he wrote was Christian. He managed musical staffs at his churches and he taught Christian education. He was not an ordained pastor, yet the degree of his daily study and the examinations he was obliged to pass proved him the peer of clergy. He was indeed one of the most equipped and effective "preachers" of his age.

Humble about his gifts, and determined that all his music was unto the Lord, we can see, as he surely did, that the *Orchestral Suites* and the *Brandenburg Concertos* and the *Musical Offering* and the *Goldberg Variations* and the suites for harpsichord and cello and violin and flute and lute—and the toccatas and trios and passacaglias and fantasias and fugues—were all merely spiritual compositions. Without words.

Is this not the perfect blueprint for any Christian? Willing to forsake worldly acclaim, this modest servant of his Savior thanked God for the talents with which he was mightily blessed and used them for the propagation of the gospel, the souls of his fellow man, and the glory of God.

The glory of God alone.

Soli Deo Gloria.

The devil does not need all the good tunes to himself.

—Martin Luther

APPENDIX A

THE FAMILY OF
JOHANN SEBASTIAN BACH

Many Bachs are significant in musical history, in the life and career of Johann Sebastian, and in this book. The text identifies and delineates them clearly. Bach had so many musical ancestors and cousins, and so many musical children, that the biography of a certain fictional composer "discovered" by the clever satirist—and, in truth, brilliant musicologist—Peter Schickele, is almost plausible. "Johann Sebastian Bach had twenty-odd children," Professor Schickele of the University of Southern North Dakota at Hoople said. "P. D. Q. Bach was the last, and the oddest." The real Bach became the launching pad for many similar *entre-nous* musical jests—not that there's anything wrong with that. For the purpose of this appendix and its usefulness for readers of this book, however, only Johann Sebastian Bach's wives and surviving children are listed here. To cite more would open Pandora's "Bachs."

WIVES AND CHILDREN REFERRED
TO IN TEXT:

Bach married his second cousin Maria Barbara Bach (1684–1720) in 1707. Of their seven children, four survived to adulthood:

Catharina Dorothea (1708–1774)
Wilhelm Friedemann (1710–1784)
Carl Philipp Emanuel (1714–1788)
Johann Gottfried Bernhard (1715–1739)

Bach married Anna Magdalena Wülcken (1701–1760) in 1721. They had thirteen children, six of whom survived to adulthood:

Gottfried Heinrich (1724–1763)
Elisabeth Juliana Friederica ("Liesgen") (1726–1781)
Johann Christoph Friedrich, the "Bückeburg" Bach
    (1732–1795)
Johann Christian, the "London Bach" (1735–1782)
Johanna Carolina (1737–1781)
Regina Susanna (1742–1809)

APPENDIX B:

CHRONOLOGY

RESIDENCES AND EMPLOYMENT OF
JOHANN SEBASTIAN BACH

1685   born in Eisenach, 21 March, in the German region of Thuringia

1695   moves to Ohrdruf to live with elder brother Johann Christoph

1700   moves to Lüneburg, attends St. Michael's School

1703   after brief work in Weimar, appointed organist at New Church in Arnstadt

1707   organist at St. Blasius Church, Mühlhausen

1708   court organist and chief chamber musician, Ducal court of Sachsen-Weimar

1717   *Kapellmeister* at Cöthen

1723   appointed cantor at St. Thomas Church in Leipzig, director of music at Thomasschule and three other Leipzig churches; holds posts until death

1736   appointed honorary court composer to the Elector of Saxony

1747   accepts invitation to perform and improvise at court of Frederick the Great, Potsdam

1750   died in Leipzig, 28 July

APPENDIX C

ANNOTATED GLOSSARY OF MUSICAL TERMS
AND FORMS USED BY BACH

Basso Continuo. Simply the "continual bass line," but in Baroque music, much more. As Bach taught—he inherited this method and perfected it—the "ground" or foundation of melodic work can be found in the bass line and built upward. But this is more than achieving a pattern of harmony notes to a bass melody. In Baroque music the notated musical score presents numbers with the bass notes, indicating full harmonies. In this manner the foundation "voice," whether choral, keyboard, organ, or strings, presents a lush, worked-out harmony. Thus all other parts are supported and endless vistas of harmonics are possible, as those parts answer in kind, in harmony, in part, in countermelodies, or—as Bach would do for dramatic emphasis—would hold back their roles when a text's essence could receive focus, for instance when a Passion would relate the death of Jesus.

BWV. The German initials for the catalog numbering of Bach's works, *Bach-Werke-Verzeichnis.*

chamber music. Ensemble music played in a room (French, *chambre*; Italian, *camera*), not necessitating a concert hall. Performance groups today sometimes double or triple the instrumentation and perform, say, the *Brandenburg Concertos* with twenty or more instruments. Yet modest ensembles of six to ten players, including soloists, played many of the concertos of Bach, Vivaldi, and Händel.

chorale. As explained more fully in the text, the chorale has evolved through the centuries in the Catholic and Lutheran churches from unaccompanied choral songs of the liturgy to complex harmonic independent pieces. Sometimes accompanied by instruments, under Bach the chorale bore no constraints of length or structure, perhaps the musical precursor of free verse. Under Bach they assumed and imparted a new function: relying on familiar church music or hymn tunes and lending the worship service a scriptural motif though music.

clavier; clavichord. The clavichord is a keyboard instrument wherein the strings are plucked; therefore it's related to the harpsichord. Today the word *clavier* is most associated with Bach's *Well-Tempered Clavier*, which referred to the tuning of the temperamental instrument, not the mood of the player. Bach likely performed this work on an instrument we know as a harpsichord, yet he owned many variations of keyboard instruments, including at least one of his own invention. He also consulted with early manufacturers of keyboard instruments that struck their strings with felt-wrapped hammers, enabling dynamic possibilities of soft (piano) and loud (forte) music—hence the name "pianoforte."

concerto. As codified by Italian middle-Baroque composers, particularly Antonio Vivaldi, the concerto (sometimes concerto grosso) is a three-movement piece, generally fast-slow-fast, featuring one or more solo instruments whose play alone, in contrast, or integrated with the full orchestra (*tutti*) provides for dynamic expression.[1] Bach was to write concertos for one to four harpsichords and for other instruments. Händel wrote eighteen concerti grossi for purely instrumental ensembles and notable concertos with organ. Mozart (especially), Haydn, and Beethoven ultimately wrote the definitive formal Classical concertos, a distinguishing characteristic of which was the improvised cadenza offered the solo performer, usually toward the end of each movement.

counterpoint. As explained more fully in the text, the term that encompasses the bass-foundation, the melodic lines above, and the ultimate harmony of seemingly independent "voices" to produce a unified piece of music. The mature form of what developed in Western music as polyphony, literally "many sounds," and whose manifestations were found in Baroque music and most typically in Bach, the fugue, the canon, and so forth.

fugue. Elementary music teachers often explain the fugue with "Row, Row, Row Your Boat," which repeats musical phrases after intervals, as fugues in fact do. But as the repeated phrases are in the same key, it technically is a canon. Fugues become complicated—and wondrous—when new themes, not just a repeated original theme, are introduced. Theoretically, an infinite number of musical phrases can be part of a fugue, but usually four or five suffice. Their employment in upward or downward variations, "mirrored" order, harmonic inversions, and so forth, can threaten cacophony but result in pleasing sounds and awesome harmonies.

harpsichord. A keyboard instrument whose strings are plucked by jacks, quills, or plectrums, producing sounds ranging from soft and lutelike—indeed the genesis of the instrument was the horizontal and mechanical playing of lute- and lyrelike harp constructions—to sharp and piercing. The harpsichord's perceived shortcoming was its lack of dynamic range—keys pressed lightly or boldly would produce the same decibel level—yet such was mitigated by elaborate harpsichords with several keyboards, organlike stops that muffled the strings, and so forth.

liturgy. The form and order of the worship service. Since the Renaissance it has evolved, especially after the Reformation when Catholics and Lutherans alike were sensitive to the needs and responses of worshipers. Under

Bach the liturgy became an invariable foundation upon which were built inventive and inspiring spiritual adornments week after week. In the eyes of some Christians, the liturgy in recent generations has become stultified in ritual and repetition.

Mass. The Catholic worship service from which the Lutheran and Protestant services evolved—perhaps the least contentious differences between the faiths. Luther retained much of the Mass, and Bach was comfortable writing the *B minor Mass* for the Elector of Saxony, in whose court Bach held an honorary position.

motet. The motet can be seen as the church's bridge between the ancient chant and the cantata; longer than chorales or hymns, much shorter than the Mass and not dramatized like Passions. It first appeared in the early thirteenth century, a small ensemble of voices. It was the beginning of the end of "plainsong," which is music without elaborate parts or harmonies; and so the motet marks the advent of polyphony—although, for a couple of centuries, rather crude. Three voices predominated—four-part harmony was not a primary instinct of Western music—and the harmonies frequently were three-five chords or open fifths, very basic. Eventually the form evolved. Counterpoint, a strong bass line, asserted itself, and the motet was incorporated into the Mass and occasionally the Lutheran service, sometimes as a multimovement introduction, on topic, to the major concert music of the service.

By its reliance on harmony, the motet provided a bridge to the development of counterpoint and figured-bass writing, thence to the fugue. By its obvious reliance on text, it hastened the development of the oratorio and cantata. Interestingly, the most innovative motet composers might have been Michael Bach and Johann Christoph Bach, uncles of Johann Sebastian, who mastered the chorale-motet and developed the cantata form. Their motets were not just beautiful, but beautifully meditative.[2]

The motet never seemed to evolve toward a permanent identity of its own, as other forms tended to serve whatever purpose it might have had. By its evolution, Spitta wrote, "the form of the motet became a very uncertain one, and when . . . the definitions of opera, oratorio, and sacred cantata were established, and the art of organ-playing reached its full development, it almost entirely lost its distinguishing characteristics."[3]

Its final distinguishing characteristic, however, should have earned it a better fate or a longer life. The motet became invariably an *a cappella* work and usually of several movements. Like brief vocal chorales, motets could provide balm to the ears and souls of listeners. Bach's *"Jesu, meine Freude"* ("Jesus, My Joy") is the most lovely of his motets. Anachronism or not, the sound of simple harmonized choruses in extended, beautiful praise is sweet.

oratorio. A genre seldom employed by Bach, the oratorio is best explained as a religious opera without a stage. Drama based on biblical stories is presented employing overtures and instrumental movements, recitatives, arias, solos and choruses, and often a narrator—an orator, providing one theory of its name—or a singing narrator who stands apart from the action. Oratorios sometimes were performed outside the settings of churches. The most famous composer of Baroque oratorios is Händel, who wrote one German, two Italian, and seventeen English-language oratorios, the most famous of which is immortal: the *Messiah*.

Bach wrote three oratorios, all for church holy days: Christmas, Easter, and Ascension Day. The Christmas Oratorio was performed over the six Sundays and feast days; its opening chorus, the sinfonia *"Jauchzet, frohlocket, auf, preiset die Tage"* ("Rejoice, be joyful, come praise the day!") with its brass fanfares and timpani drums, is one of the most rousing movements in all of music.

Passion. The Passion is basically an oratorio with a more dedicated theme—the suffering and death of the Savior—and more drama, action, and even costumes on occasion. Presented during the apogee of the church year, Passions often unfolded over several evenings during Holy Week, specially integrated into the liturgy.

Traditionally, composers were free to be as creative and artistic as possible. They could use a libretto drawn from biblical texts, familiar writings of the church, newly written words, in any combination. The music—presumably because the Easter story summed up Christ's mission and ministry—was allowed to be drawn from various sources, whether other composers, or the composer's earlier music called "parodies" (not in the sense of humor, but of reworking), or completely fresh music.

Passions were enacted as early as the eighth century, always during Holy Week. Words of the evangelists were chanted, and words of Jesus and other principal players were spoken. In the early sixteenth century, the church in Holland set the entire Passion-week story to music. Luther heard it, approved, and had his friends Walther and Melanchthon publish it, with words in German and Latin.

There are famous Passions of our time. A renowned Passion play is produced in Oberammergau, a small Bavarian town of two thousand inhabitants, half of whom stage and act in the seven-hour re-creation of Holy Week events. The play has been produced every ten years since 1634 when the town, threatened by the bubonic plague, collectively prayed for mercy and vowed to share with the world this portion of the gospel story if they were spared.

In Drumheller, Alberta, Canada, every July the Canadian Badlands Passion Play is presented in a thirty-acre canyon bowl that forms a natural amphitheater.

Many people watched the recent Mel Gibson movie *The Passion of the Christ*.

The first German musical Passions were sweet, dramatic, and moving in their antique structure, the entire productions emoting holiness even when words were not understood.[4] When the Italian opera attracted many German audiences, and since Passions were so close in form to operas, the German presentations, including Bach's, adopted spectacular scope: a full orchestra, large choirs, freer expression. There was another reason for the bling. As operas and musical theaters grew coarser, churches wanted to retain and deliver purity for the masses.

In another story of frenzied crowds excited by a performance of Baroque church music, there were reports that people had to be calmed and turned away from a performance of Händel's *Passion*—text by Brockes—possibly conducted by Bach himself. The performance was criticized in some quarters as vulgar for its graphic depictions of Christ's tortured scourging[5]—a foreshadowing of the criticism of Mel Gibson's movie!

Bach's surviving Passions are the *St. Matthew*, which he considered one of his lifetime's greatest works, and the *St. John*. At least three others have been lost.

We made an earlier reference to Heinrich Ignaz Franz von Biber's polychoral Masses in the cavernous Salzburg Cathedral. Bach employed the same "surround-sound" structure in the *St. Matthew Passion* and the grand *Magnificat*—stereophony. At St. Thomas Church, certain movements were performed from the east organ loft, the "swallow's nest" opposite the main musician's gallery at the west end of the church, a double-choir structure "that produced a splendid and festive effect."[6]

The structure of Bach's Passions was strictly traditional; he changed little of the form he inherited. The straight biblical narrative was distributed among soloists (evangelists and various *soliloquentes*, or individual speakers, including Jesus, Peter, Pilate) and choirs (various *turbae* or crowds, including high priests, Roman soldiers, Jews).[7] The Passion's flow was dotted by narration, hymn strophes, and contemplative lyrics, "madrigal pieces" of free verse, mainly delivered as arias. One can begin to appreciate the spectacle that audiences beheld: a combination of church and theater, Greek-style drama and opera, music and voice, costume and acting.

Bach revised the *St. Matthew Passion* several times through the years. His best works were repeated in his churches and performed elsewhere, just as he occasionally performed works of esteemed contemporaries. Of his manuscript scores that survive today, none bears such respect as *St. Matthew*. In 1736, at least, he considered it his most significant work.[8] His autograph score shows loving attention, written in red or brown inks according to the biblical and dramatic libretto sources and employing calligraphy in careful Gothic or Latin letters. It was preserved as an heirloom. It appears that a later accident, perhaps a spill, damaged portions of some pages and Bach lovingly repaired those sections with paste-overs.[9]

This was the same care that the early evangelists, or recipients of their epistles, might have shown to those texts. It is notable that history came to call Bach "The Fifth Evangelist," the accolade bypassing even his spiritual mentor Martin Luther.

NOTES

CHAPTER 1

1. Thence to take hold in Anglo-Saxon Britain and cross the Atlantic Ocean to America. Hubert Howe Bancroft and Frederick Jackson Turner were the chief proponents of this theory that posited philosophic determinism more than cultural evolution; particularly Turner in his seminal paper "The Significance of the Frontier in American History," delivered to the American Historical Association in 1893 at the World's Columbian Exposition.
2. Much of this chapter's material on everyday life and changing social norms is drawn from the essays in *A History of Private Life* by Philippe Ariès.
3. Ariès, *Private Life*, 71.
4. Ariès, *Private Life*, 102 et seq. As a typical and devout Lutheran of his time.
5. Ariès, *Private Life*, 104. These are descriptions of generic Lutheran practices of the seventeenth century, written by historians Roger Chartier, Yves Castan, and François Lebrun, who studied the Lutherans of Alsace and the adjacent German and French lands. We can assume that some of the rites are similar to the Lutherans of Thuringia and Saxony.
6. Jones, "Bach and Musical Hermeneutics."

CHAPTER 2

1. Wolff, *Bach: The Learned Musician*, 13.
2. Jones, "Bach and Musical Hermeneutics," supra.
3. Schweitzer, *J. S. Bach*, 1:5.
4. Ibid., 1:76.
5. Ariès, *Private Life*, 118.
6. Ibid., 132–33.
7. Jones, "Bach and Musical Hermeneutics," op. cit.
8. Ibid.

CHAPTER 3

1. Forkel, *Bach: His Life, Art, and Work*, passim. Sebastian Bach, in the 1730s, began to collect documents about his family's history, a project whose continuation by sons Wilhelm Friedemann and especially Carl Philipp Emanuel leaves posterity indebted. These papers, and the assistance of C. P. E. Bach, aided Forkel in the publication of the first biography of J. S. Bach in 1802, spawning the "rehabilitation" that has not ceased and only grown ever since. The biographical aspects of this chapter largely are drawn from Forkel's account.
2. Schweitzer, *J. S. Bach*, 1:97.
3. Cahill, *How the Irish Saved Civilization*, 195–207.
4. Wolff, *Bach: The Learned Musician*, 30.
5. Ibid., 49.
6. Ibid., 26.
7. Ibid., 38–39.
8. Schweitzer, *J. S. Bach*, 1:100.
9. Ibid., 1:52–54 passim.
10. Spitta, *Bach: His Work and Influence*, 1:337.
11. Ibid., 2:19–21; Schweitzer, *J. S. Bach*, 1:110.

CHAPTER 4

1. Schweitzer, *J. S. Bach*, 1:113–115.
2. Leaver, roundtable discussion.
3. Ibid.
4. Ibid.
5. Fleischer, "Bach and the Organ" in Nickel, *Little Bach Book*, passim.
6. Schweitzer, *J. S. Bach*, 1:39–40.
7. Nettl, "Bach the Teacher" in Nickel, *Little Bach Book*, 26–27.
8. Schweitzer, *J. S. Bach*, 126–31. These descriptions are from Bach himself (notes he scribbled on the first page of his score of the cantata *Nun kommt der Heiden Heiland*) and research of Albert Schweitzer, Bach's biographer and Lutheran organist. I have here preserved and incorporated some of Schweitzer's personalized characterizations of "backstage" at the church.

9. Spitta, *Bach: His Work and Influence*, 2:279.

10. Schweitzer, *J. S. Bach*, supra.

11. Wolff, *Bach: The Learned Musician*, 251.

12. Leaver, roundtable discussion, *op cit.*

13. Urfer, *A Life Worth Living*. A video production imagining a family reunion provides an utterly charming, genuine, and trustworthy portrayal of the family life of the Bachs.

14. Forkel, *Bach: His Life, Art, and Work*, 6 et seq.

15. Ibid., 424.

16. Snyder, "Bach: Orthodox Lutheran Theologian?"

17. Wolff, *Bach: The Learned Musician*, 8.

18. Quoted in Schweitzer, *J. S. Bach*, 1:115.

19. Leaver, roundtable discussion, op. cit.

20. Ibid.

21. Huneker, "Bach—Once, Last, All the Time" in *Old Fogy*, 92. Huneker (1857–1921), seminal influence on H. L. Mencken, Benjamin de Casseres, Vance Thompson, Gilbert Seldes, and others is in the estimation of this book's author the greatest American critic in fields other than music as well. Through his career he contributed to the Philadelphia *Ledger*; *Étude* magazine; *The Musical Courier*; *Puck* magazine; the New York *Sun*; *The New York Times*; and the New York *World*, among other publications.

22. Ibid., 87.

23. Huneker, "A Mood Reactionary" in *Variations*, 241.

CHAPTER 5

1. Fleischer in Nickel, *Little Bach Book*, 77–78.

2. Nettl in Nickel, *Little Bach Book*, 27–29 et seq.

3. Ibid., supra.

4. Forkel, *Bach: His Life, Art, and Work*, 93–104, offers profiles of many Bach students, some of whom achieved prominence in the church and in music.

5. Ibid., passim.

6. Quoted in Holmes, *Life of Mozart*.

7. Wolff, *Bach: The Learned Musician*, 4.

8. Quoted in David, *The New Bach Reader*, 305–6.

9. Einstein, *Greatness in Music*, 213.
10. Schweitzer, *J. S. Bach*, 1:55.
11. Spitta, *Bach: His Work and Influence*, 1:461.

Chapter 6

1. Robert K. Wallace briefly but brilliantly discusses this observation in his comparison of music and literature of the Classical period—overall a valuable and unfortunately neglected consideration of similitude in the arts: solo/*tutti* in concertos and individual verses society in fiction; etc. Wallace, *Jane Austen and Mozart*, 34 et seq.
2. Ibid.
3. Levitin, *Your Brain on Music*, passim.
4. Wolff, *Bach: The Learned Musician*, 278.
5. Ibid., 417 et seq.
6. Ibid., 8.
7. Schweitzer, *J. S. Bach*, 1:39–40.
8. Fleischer in Nickel, *Little Bach Book*, 62–63.
9. Forkel, *Bach: His Life, Art, and Work*, 66.
10. Quoted in David, *The New Bach Reader*, 397.
11. Fleischer in Nickel, *Little Bach Book*, 63.
12. Forkel, *Bach: His Life, Art, and Work*, 68–69.
13. Quoted by Johann Friedrich Köhler in David, *The New Bach Reader*, 412.

Chapter 7

1. Spitta, *Bach: His Work and Influence*, 1:414.
2. Ibid., 3:62–63.
3. The author will intrude with his own preference on such a question. Hermann Scherchen, the German conductor, arranged a very idiosyncratic version—perhaps consistent with Bach's intentions—and recorded *The Art of the Fugue* with solo harpsichord, strings, wind ensemble, etc., different scoring, movement by movement. It is powerful and haunting, beautiful in its complexity, evocative of the faceted genius of Bach.

4. Einstein, *Greatness in Music*, 123–25 (emphasis added).

5. Ibid., supra.

6. Wolff, *Bach: The Learned Musician*, 426–31.

7. Fleischer in Nickel, *Little Bach Book*, 78.

8. Ibid.

9. Peter Billam, *Vor deinen Thron tret' ich hiermit*, piano arrangement and essay, www.pjb.com.au/mus/free/thron_kbd.pdf (accessed October 27, 2009).

10. Einstein, *Greatness in Music*, 282.

11. Research in the 1930s revealed that it was more than boyhood eyestrain that damaged Bach's eyes. Although the cause and actual malady remain unknown, it seems likely that Bach's eyes were mistreated; also that he might have suffered infection or eventual death at the hands of the doctor. See Lenth, "Bach and the English Oculist," 182–98.

12. A superb description of Bach and his eye troubles—summarizing past discoveries and offering learned speculation—is provided by H. C. Zegers, MD: "The Eyes of Johann Sebastian Bach" in *Archives of Ophthalmology* 23, no. 19 (October 2005): 1427–30, from which pertinent facts here are drawn.

13. Einstein, *Greatness in Music*, 281.

14. Said, "Cosmic Ambition" in *London Review of Books*, 11–14.

15. Leaver, roundtable discussion, op. cit.

Chapter 8

1. Luther, "On Baptism," paragraph CCCLIII.

2. Kretzmann, "Bach and the 20th Century" in Nickel, *Little Bach Book*, 3.

3. Leaver, roundtable discussion, op. cit.

4. Quoted in Kupferberg, *Basically Bach*, 7–8.

5. Leaver, roundtable discussion, op. cit.

6. The illustration appears in David, *The New Bach Reader*, 374.

7. Romijn, liner notes booklet.

8. Huneker, "The Royal Road to Parnassus" in *Mezzotints*. This was Huneker's first collection of essays; *Variations* was his last.

9. Ibid., 284.

10. Mencken, *Mencken on Music*, 19 et seq.
11. Taylor, *Fantasia*, 20–21.
12. Ruber, *Bach and the Heavenly Choir*, passim.
13. Kretzmann in Nickel, *Little Bach Book*, 2.

APPENDIX C

1. The musical satirist Peter Schickele emphasized the occasionally less complementary relationship between *solo* and *tutti* in his composition "Concerto for Piano versus Orchestra."
2. Spitta, *Bach: His Work and Influence*, 1:55–84.
3. Ibid., 59.
4. Schweitzer, *J. S. Bach*, 1:84.
5. Ibid., 95.
6. Wolff, *Bach: The Learned Musician*, 289.
7. Ibid., 291 et seq presents a vivid picture of the dramatic scope of these Passion presentations.
8. Ibid., 298.
9. Ibid.

BIBLIOGRAPHY

Adams, Henry. *Mont-Saint-Michel and Chartres*. Boston and New York: Houghton Mifflin, 1913.

Ariés, Philippe. *A History of Private Life. Volume 3: Passions of the Renaissance*. Edited by Roger Chartier. Translated by Arthur Goldhammer. Cambridge and London: Belknap Press of Harvard University Press, 1989.

The Bach Cantata Web Site. Hosted by Aryeh Oron. http://www.bach-cantatas.com.

Cahill, Thomas. *How the Irish Saved Civilization*. New York: Anchor Books, 1996.

David, Hans T., and Arthur Mendel, eds. *The New Bach Reader: A Life of Johann Sebastian Bach in Letters and Documents*. Revised and expanded by Christoph Wolff. New York: W. W. Norton, 1998.

Einstein, Alfred. *Greatness in Music*. Translated by César Saerchinger. New York, London, Toronto: Oxford University Press, 1941.

Forkel, Johann Nikolaus. *Johann Sebastian Bach: His Life, Art, and Work*. Translated with notes and appendices by Charles Sanford Terry. London: Constable and Company, 1920.

Grove, Sir George, et al. *Grove's Dictionary of Music and Musicians*. Edited by H. C. Colles. 3rd ed. New York: Macmillan, 1948.

Holmes, Edward. *The Life of Mozart, Including His Correspondence*. London: Chapman and Hall, 1845.

Huneker, James. *Mezzotints in Modern Music*. New York: Charles Scribner's Sons, 1899.

———. *Old Fogy: His Musical Opinions and Grotesques*. Philadelphia: Theodore Presser Co., 1913.

———. *Variations*. New York: Charles Scribner's Sons, 1921.

Jones, Paul S. "J. S. Bach and Musical Hermeneutics: An Evangelical Composer/Preacher." *Singing and Making Music: Issues in Church*

Music Today. Philadelphia: P&R Publishing, 2006. http://home. comcast.net/~pjones25/articles/Bach_Hermeneutics.htm (accessed October 27, 2009).

J. S. Bach Home Page. Hosted by Jan Hanford (North America) and Jan Koster (Europe). http://www.jsbach.org.

Kupferberg, Herbert. *Basically Bach: A 300th Birthday Celebration*. London: Robson Books, 1985.

Leaver, Robin, et al. *Bach, the Evangelist*. Roundtable discussion on *Encounter*. Radio National / Australian Broadcasting Corporation program, October 22, 2000. Featuring Robin Leaver, John Kleinig, and Michael Marissen.

Lenth, Bert. "Bach and the English Oculist." In *Music and Letters*, a periodical publication of Oxford University Press, 1938, XIX(2):182–98.

Levitin, Daniel J. *This Is Your Brain on Music*. New York: Plume Book/ Penguin Group, 2006.

Luther, Martin. *Colloquia Mensalia* [The Table Talk of Martin Luther]. Translated by William Hazlitt, Esq. Philadelphia: The Lutheran Publication Society / Center for Reformed Theology, 1997. http:// www.reformed.org/master/index.html?mainframe=/documents/ Table_talk/table_talk.html (accessed December 1, 2009).

Mencken, H. L. *H. L. Mencken on Music*. Selected and edited by Louis Cheslock. New York: Alfred A. Knopf, 1961.

Nickel, Theodore Hoelty, ed. *The Little Bach Book*. Valparaiso: Valparaiso University Press, 1950.

Polisensky, J. V. "The Thirty Years' War and the Crises and Revolutions of Seventeenth-Century Europe." *Past and Present* 39 (1968).

Regnery, Henry. *Memoirs of a Dissident Publisher*. Chicago: Regnery Books, 1985.

Rilling, Helmuth, artistic director. *The Complete Works of Johann Sebastian Bach*. Stuttgart: Internationale Bachakademie / Neuhausen: Hänssler Classic, 1999.

Romijn, Clemens. Liner notes booklet accompanying "The Complete Works of Johann Sebastian Bach." *Bach Edition*. Brilliant Classics. www.brilliantclassics.com.

Ruber, Johannes. *Bach and the Heavenly Choir*. Translated from the

German by Maurice Michael. Cleveland: World Publishing, 1956.

Said, Edward. "Cosmic Ambition." Book review in *London Review of Books* 23, no. 14 (July 19, 2001).

Schweitzer, Albert. *J. S. Bach*. Translated by Ernest Newman. New York: Macmillan, 1950.

Snyder, Rev. Walter. "J. S. Bach: Orthodox Lutheran Theologian?" Paper prepared for European Lutheranism course, Concordia Seminary, St. Louis, MO. http://www.xrysostom.com/bach.html (accessed December 10, 2009).

Spitta, Philipp. *Johann Sebastian Bach: His Work and Influence on the Music of Germany, 1685–1750*. Translated from the German by Clara Bell and J. A. Fuller-Maitland. London: Novello & Co. / New York: Dover Publications, 1951.

Taylor, Deems. *Walt Disney's Fantasia*. Foreword by Leopold Stowkowski. New York: Simon and Schuster, 1940.

Trautmann, Christoph. "J. S. Bach: New Light on His Faith" in *Concordia Theological Monthly* 42 (1971).

Urfer, Pamela, writer and executive producer. *A Life Worth Living: J.S. Bach's 60th Birthday Party*. Peter Homer, director. Video. Purfer Productions, 2000.

Wallace, Robert K. *Jane Austen and Mozart: Classical Equilibrium in Fiction and Music*. Athens: University of Georgia Press, 1983.

Wolff, Christoph. *Johann Sebastian Bach: The Learned Musician*. New York: W. W. Norton, 2000.

Zegers, H. C. "The Eyes of Johann Sebastian Bach." *Archives of Ophthalmology* 23, no. 19 (October 2005): 1427–430.

ACKNOWLEDGMENTS

I t is a challenge to write about music and a composer without being able to provide earphones to readers. But it is easy to write of a great person's great faith . . . and it is a great privilege. The following people have assisted me in word, deed, and prayer.

Diane Obbema has been my prayer partner on this project, and her support has greatly encouraged me along the way. Fred and Marion Horn were invaluable helpers, correcting my German, informing my geography and history, and testing my points of view. I never drove either to the point of saying, *"Ich habe genug,"* and they were always patient and forthcoming. I also thank Rev. John Siegmund of Kreuzkirche in Ulzburg, Germany. John is an old college friend who devoted special attention to this manuscript. His input was essential. I thank Herr Bach for reacquainting us.

My daughter and son-in-law, Emily and Norman McCorkell, students at the Irish Bible Institute, read and reread the manuscript. In the midst of studies and a baby on the way, they were always helpful with advice, corrections, and, again, testing my points of view. This sort of input an author covets and is blessed to receive. Also I felt helped by the inspiration and example of my late cousin Robert Beisacher and the enthusiasms of Roy Relph, David Wunsch, and Michael Goldberg;

also Ken Tobin and Mike Pikosky of the Classical Music Union of the American University, Washington DC.

I am grateful for the prayerful as well as logistical support of Ted Marschall, Heather and Pat Shaw, Marlene Bagnull, Hope Flinchbaugh, Becky Spencer, Mark Dittmar, Gary Groth, Jon Barli, Corey Madson, Patrick Mitchel, Tom Heintjes, Debbie Hardy, Pastor Waldemar Makus of the Swartz Creek German Church of God, C. Putnam Basbas, Eduoard Norton, and Ivan Smith of the Swartz Creek Perkins Library.

With all these acknowledgments, I share the credit for whatever information and insights might strike the reader's attention, but responsibility for any mistakes, and all the points of view, are mine.

Any author would be grateful—I surely am—for editors as perspicacious and creative as Thomas Nelson's Kristen Parrish and Heather Skelton. My literary representative, Greg Johnson of WordServe Literary Agency, has been supportive and encouraging from the start. I greatly value his guidance.

ABOUT THE AUTHOR

Rick Marschall has written or edited more than sixty books and many magazine articles. His two areas principally have been popular culture and the Christian field. In 2000, *Bostonia Magazine* called him "perhaps America's foremost authority on popular culture."

He has been a political cartoonist, newspaper columnist, magazine editor, book publisher, teacher, and lecturer. He was an editor with several newspaper syndicates and with Marvel Comics. He has written for Walt Disney comics and has written four books on country music and two books on television history. Marschall is contributing editor of *Hogan's Alley* magazine and managing director of Rosebud Archives, a vintage-image resource company. He is also president of Marschall Books, specializing in cartoon history and anthologies.

In the Christian field, Marschall has written many devotionals and the "answer book," *The Secret Revealed*, with Dr. Jim Garlow (FaithWords, 2007). He served as director of product development for Youth Specialties, a youth-ministry resource company.

Marschall has taught at several colleges: The School of Visual Arts in New York City, Philadelphia College of Art (now University of the Arts), Rutgers University, and the Summer Institute for the Gifted at Bryn Mawr University.

As a lifelong devotee of Baroque music, and Bach in particular, Marschall has attended two Bach festivals in Europe, and commemorations in Augsburg, Germany, on the five hundredth anniversary of Martin Luther's birth.

Monday Morning Music Ministry is a weekly blog of devotions keyed to hymns, songs, and Christian music. Marschall has been writing it for two years, and it is carried regularly by www.RealClearReligion.org and ASSIST News Service www.ASSISTNews.net . Marschall's blog is www.RickMarschallArts.com.

Marschall was the 2008 recipient of Christian Writer of the Year award from the Greater Philadelphia Christian Writers Conference. He and his wife live in Swartz Creek, Michigan.

Close Encounters of the Christian Kind

— Available Now —

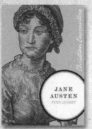

JANE AUSTEN
9781595553027

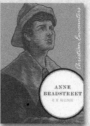

ANNE BRADSTREET
9781595551092

WILLIAM F. BUCKLEY
9781595550651

JOHN BUNYAN
9781595553041

WINSTON CHURCHILL
9781595553065

ISAAC NEWTON
9781595553034

SAINT FRANCIS
9781595551078

SAINT PATRICK
9781595553058

D. L. MOODY
9781595550477

SAINT NICHOLAS
9781595551153

SERGEANT YORK
9781595550255

GALILEO
9781595550316

Available August 2011

GEORGE WASHINGTON CARVER
9781595553034

J.R.R. TOLKIEN
9781595551078